From East and West:

*Regional Views
on Reconfederation*

*Norman Cameron, E.J. Chambers,
Derek Hum, John McCallum,
Doug May, M.B. Percy,
Dane Rowlands, Wayne Simpson*

The Canada Round:
A Series on the Economics of
Constitutional Renewal — No. 6

John McCallum, Series Editor

C.D. Howe Institute

C.D. Howe Institute publications are available from:

Renouf Publishing Company Limited, 1294 Algoma Road,
Ottawa, Ontario K1B 3W8; phone (613) 741-4333; fax (613) 741-5439

and from Renouf's stores at:

61 Sparks Street, Ottawa (613) 238-8985
211 Yonge Street, Toronto (416) 363-3171

For trade book orders, please contact:

McGraw-Hill Ryerson Limited, 300 Water Street,
Whitby, Ontario L1N 9B6; phone (416) 430-5050

Institute publications are also available in microform from:

Micromedia Limited, 165 Hôtel de Ville, Place du Portage, Phase II,
Hull, Quebec J8X 3X2

This book is printed on recycled, acid-free paper.

Canadian Cataloguing in Publication Data

Main entry under title:

From east and west : regional views on reconfederation

(The Canada round ; no. 6)
ISBN 0-88806-291-5

1. Canada – Economic conditions – 1971–   .
2. Canada – Economic conditions – Regional disparities.*
3. Federal government – Canada. I. Cameron, Norman E.
II. C.D. Howe Institute. III. Series.

HC115.F76 1991   330.971   C92-093053-0

© C.D. Howe Institute, Toronto.
Quotation with appropriate credit is permissible.
Printed and bound in Canada by Hignell Printing Limited,
Winnipeg, Manitoba, December 1991.

Contents

Foreword

Canada appears poised to embark on an historic political recon-figuration. It is essential that this process be undertaken with a clear and widely diffused understanding of the well-spring of Canadians' economic prosperity.

It is with that in mind that the C.D. Howe Institute presents this series of monographs entitled *The Canada Round*. The series assem-bles the work of many of Canada's leading economic and political analysts. The monographs are organized into two groups. The first group, called "The Economics of Constitutional Renewal", rests on the assumption of renewed federalism and is organized around economic themes. It examines the economic goals that Canadians have set for themselves, as well as the means of achieving them and the influence of alternative constitutional structures.

The second group of studies, called "The Economics of the Breakup of Confederation", examines the economic consequences of Quebec independence for both Quebec and the rest of Canada. A unique feature of the "Breakup" studies is that they are integrated with the research that has already been carried out by Quebec's Bélanger-Campeau Commission. Where appropriate, each of the studies in this group includes a summary of the relevant analysis by the Bélanger-Campeau Commission, contributions by experts from across Canada, as well as shorter critiques or replies. This format, we believe, will help to pierce Canada's "several solitudes" and create a pan-Canadian meeting of minds.

The Canada Round is not intended to alarm or frighten — the process of collective political definition in this country will turn on more than simply questions of dollars and cents. And, as these monographs will reveal, economics rarely produces an open-and-shut case as to the superiority of one possible set of rules over another. Even if it could do this, it would be unwise to assume that economic analysis alone could change the minds of those who are already committed to a particular vision of the political future.

It is equally clear, however, that Canadians are now seeking a greater understanding of the links between the economy, the Constitution, and legal and political life. A significant reform of the Constitution will influence the economy, in some cases for the better; a rending of the Constitution under conditions of acrimony will almost certainly damage it. Thus, the purpose of the series is to help Canadians think constructively about the benefits and costs of alternative constitutional designs.

Underlying the series is a focus on the economic well-being of Canadians, now and in the future. To best insure this well-being over the short run, Canada needs calm, open negotiations in which efforts are made to understand and incorporate the aspirations of all the participants. This series of monographs is dedicated to that effort.

John McCallum, the series editor and Chairman of the Department of Economics at McGill University, organized the intellectual input. Within the C.D. Howe Institute, David Brown, Senior Policy Analyst, played a coordinating role. This sixth monograph in the series was copy edited by Lenore d'Anjou, Heather Lange, and Barry A. Norris, and desktop published by Brenda Palmer. As with all C.D. Howe Institute publications, the analysis and views presented here are the responsibility of the authors and do not necessarily reflect the opinions of the Institute's members or Board of Directors.

Thomas E. Kierans
President and
Chief Executive Officer

The Study in Brief

This volume, the sixth in the C.D. Howe Institute's *The Canada Round* series, provides perspectives on the economics of constitutional renewal from Atlantic Canada and Western Canada.

Doug May and Dane Rowlands describe the high dependence of Atlantic Canada on federal government financial assistance, suggesting that, for various reasons, the level of this assistance may be reduced in the future. They outline a number of possible adjustment mechanisms that the region might pursue in the event of such a cut in federal transfers. In general, they are pessimistic regarding the effectiveness or desirability of adjustment through usual market mechanisms. Indeed, their simulations — based on the Newfoundland economy — indicate that the total elimination of net federal transfers could result in a 50 percent reduction in population, or a 40 percent drop in per capita income, or some combination of the two.

In their study from the perspective of Western Canada, Edward Chambers and Michael Percy begin by documenting the extreme dependence of the region on a small number of exported commodities. This, they show, results in an extraordinarily volatile economy and great susceptibility to harassment of Western Canadian interests by U.S. protectionism. Given this analysis, they argue, Western Canada derives two major economic benefits from Confederation. First, Canada has more clout in international trade relations than would an independent Western Canada. Second, the economic stabilization and insurance aspects of an economic union are crucial for the West. Major benefits under this heading include the more diversified tax base of Canada as a whole, the ability to pool risks over a larger population, and the safety valve provided by the ability of people to move freely into the region and out of it, depending on the state of the Western Canadian economy and the availability of jobs. In some cases, however, these benefits from the economic union have been potential rather than realized, since federal policies have not always operated to stabilize the region's economy.

"The West" is far from being a homogeneous region — in particular, British Columbia and Alberta are substantially richer than Saskatchewan and Manitoba. Norman Cameron, Derek Hum, and Wayne Simpson provide a perspective from the "less-affluent" West. In general, they argue, people from Manitoba and Saskatchewan are strongly committed to the principles of political equality, economic equity, and, perhaps to a lesser degree, economic efficiency.

The reader will quickly become aware that there are sharp differences in regional economic perspectives. In particular, perspectives differ on three important issues:

- the basic facts concerning the regional distribution of federal spending and revenues;
- the desirable roles of market and nonmarket forces in bringing about structural adjustment; and
- the view that the primary purpose of federal regional policies should be to help stabilize regional economies against *temporary* shocks, as opposed to the view that they should provide *permanent* net inflows of resources to the less-affluent regions.

These points emerge clearly from the short comments by Chambers and Percy on the essay by May and Rowlands, and by Rowlands on the essay by Chambers and Percy. As the final contribution to this volume, I attempt to provide an overview of the basic pattern of federal redistributive efforts, as well as a longer summary and synthesis of competing regional perspectives.

John McCallum
Series Editor

Atlantic Canada in Confederation: Uncharted Waters with Dangerous Shoals

Doug May and Dane Rowlands

International economics focuses on the interactions of two or more dissimilar economic structures. The key theoretical results of these interactions are that under conditions of perfect competition and unrestricted mobility, goods and services will be traded to exploit comparative advantage, and factors of production — labor and capital — will migrate to equalize their returns.

Dissimilar economic structures can exist within a single country as well, most significantly in those that are explicitly federal in nature. In these countries, the constitution will generally circumscribe the extent to which a free internal market in goods and factors of production is permitted to function. In addition, the constitution can provide alternative methods for transregional "equilibration". When distinct political entities surrender elements of sovereignty to a federal structure, the nature of the economic union and the regional adjustment mechanisms represent critical elements of the constitutional *quid pro quo*. Constitutional reform, therefore, requires an examination — and possibly a modification — of the "social contract" that determines the nature of the federal state.

For the four Atlantic provinces, a critical economic feature of Confederation was the protection of the local economies from the seemingly inexorable pull of Central Canada and the northeastern United States. In the absence of economic protection, the Atlantic provinces feared the loss of their manufacturing sector, employment, and eventually their population to the larger industrial centers, leaving behind a depopulated resource hinterland. Thus, Atlantic Canada gave up the right to impose restrictions on the mobility of goods and factors in return for federal policies designed to encourage further economic development in the region and a livelihood for its citizens. Federal protection of the Atlantic economy, therefore, was and is a critical constitutional *quid pro quo* in the Atlantic view of the Canadian social contract.

This paper examines the nature of the Atlantic Canadian vision of Confederation by referring to three primary routes for inter-regional equilibration: trade, transfers, and migration. The first three sections describe current structures and trends, and examine how the Atlantic economy is likely to be affected by the various constitutional reforms currently under consideration. A fourth section examines the results of simulating various constitutional scenarios with an econometric model. The final section of the paper discusses the likelihood of various constitutional reforms and presents our concluding arguments.[1]

Economic Structure and Trade

Current Atlantic Canadian Trading Patterns

The four Atlantic provinces have strikingly similar trading patterns, the most obvious similarity being the large trade deficits each province runs.[2] The overall trade deficit for Atlantic Canada in 1984 was

---

1 We would like to thank Rose Anne Devlin, John McCallum, and John Rideout for their comments and advice. We would also like to acknowledge the research and technical assistance provided by Rose Acouin, Brian Delaney, John Rideout, Sharada Weir, and Jian Zhu. Any remaining errors are, of course, our responsibility.

2 Data on interprovincial trade flows are not yet available as a regular time series. The last available data on goods and service flows are from the 1984 provincial input-output tables of Statistics Canada; these data form the basis of the discussion presented here. It should be noted that these data are far from perfect; measurement of service flows is particularly suspect. In the absence of alternatives, however, they provide the best portrait of interprovincial trade.

slightly over $7 billion, while GDP at market prices was approximately $26.3 billion.[3] The deficit-to-GDP ratios for each separate province ranged from a low of 18 percent for New Brunswick to a high of 31.6 percent for Nova Scotia; Prince Edward Island and Newfoundland recorded deficit-to-GDP ratios in the neighborhood of 29 percent.

Overall, the Atlantic region ran a trade surplus in 1984 only in the primary sector, led by forestry, mining, and fishing.[4] The only other net surpluses were in the utilities and transportation and communications sectors. Communications was the only sector for which there was a net trade surplus with the rest of Canada. Atlantic Canada's international trade was far more balanced than the region's trade with the rest of Canada; large surpluses in the primary sectors were offset by manufactured and fuel imports from overseas, resulting in a net international deficit of only $547 million.

The performances of individual provinces did not diverge significantly. Newfoundland's trade surpluses were limited to the mining, fishing, forestry, and utilities sectors, with utilities reflecting hydro-electric sales to Quebec. The international trade balance stood in surplus, with almost twice as much sold internationally than to Quebec, Ontario, the Western provinces, and the Territories combined. The international surplus was generated by high primary product exports from mining, fishing, and forestry. International imports were represented largely by manufactured metal products. Newfoundland's transportation and communications, mining, and utilities sectors were the province's major sources of exports to the rest of Canada. Imports from the rest of Canada were spread evenly between services, manufactures, and primary products and fuel.

Prince Edward Island relied mostly on fishing, agricultural, and transportation and communications surpluses to generate net sur-

---

3 The $7 billion figure is from the input-output table information presented in the Appendix. Other Statistics Canada data suggest an even higher figure ($8.7 billion) as the deficit plus a statistical discrepancy for Atlantic Canada.

4 See the Appendix for the tables used in this discussion, and to see how subsectors were grouped.

pluses and an overall international trading surplus. Exports were concentrated in these three sectors as well. Imports of manufactured goods, fuel and utilities, and other services were the major debits for the province, with trade imbalances in the first two sectors contributing the most to the overall trade deficit. The largest bilateral deficit existed with Atlantic Canada, while trade with Quebec was relatively balanced.

Nova Scotia's big trade surpluses were generated in the fishing, transportation and communications, forestry, and financial services sectors. This province also had a large international textiles surplus. Outside Atlantic Canada, however, there were surpluses only in fuel, transportation and communications, and financial services. Sales to non-Atlantic Canada were 56 percent of Nova Scotia's total exports, while 59 percent of its imports were from non-Atlantic Canada. Nova Scotia had a trade surplus only with the rest of Atlantic Canada, resulting almost exclusively from fuel exports.[5]

Similar patterns were found in New Brunswick, although its international trade deficit was small. The province recorded overall surpluses in all four primary sectors, in utilities, and in transportation and communications. Exports destined for outside the Atlantic region were fairly evenly split between Canada and the rest of the world. New Brunswick's imports of manufactured goods, fuel, and other services accounted for its overall deficit.

Finally, one study suggests that Quebec has done relatively well in exporting manufactured goods to the Atlantic provinces compared with the rest of Canada.[6] Large Quebec trading surpluses were registered in the primary, secondary, fuel and utilities, and services sectors; deficits were registered only in transportation and communications and beverages. Over 50 percent of Quebec's net surplus with Atlantic Canada was generated by its secondary industry. Atlantic Canada

---

5 Fuel exports statistics from Nova Scotia capture re-exports of fuel imported in a crude form and processed within the province.

6 See Pierre-Paul Proulx, "Primary and Secondary Trade between Canada and the United States: A National, Regional, and Provincial Overview with Particular Reference to Interregional Trade in the Borderlands," Cahier 9038 (Montreal: Université de Montréal, Département de sciences économiques, December 1990).

bought about 5 percent of Quebec's total output. In turn, Quebec bought roughly 10.5 percent of the output of Atlantic Canada.

In summary, then, Atlantic Canada performed far better internationally than it did within Canada. Total Atlantic exports were evenly split between other Canadians and the rest of the world. However, almost twice as much was imported from the rest of Canada as from overseas, resulting in an enormous trade deficit with the non-Atlantic provinces. Exports to the rest of Canada were split evenly between Quebec and the remainder of non-Atlantic Canada, while Quebec remained somewhat below Ontario and the West as a source of Canadian imports. The Atlantic provinces buy over twice as much from the rest of Canada as they sell back. This statistical summary lends some simplistic support to the proposition that Confederation has resulted in transfers to the Atlantic region that are then spent on goods produced in the rest of Canada — notably, Central Canada.[7] If there is indeed some structural bias that induces Atlantic Canadians to spend an abnormally high proportion of transfer income on imports from the rest of Canada, then donors may be inclined to view such transfers more "charitably".

Current Trading Barriers

The establishment or removal of constitutional jurisdictions are critical determinants of the "external" environment of an economy. With changes in jurisdiction comes the possibility of fewer or more barriers to trade. Hence, the constitutional future of Canada holds

---

7 It would be incorrect to suggest that transfers from the rest of Canada must be spent on imports from other provinces. Transfers could — and to a degree are — used to finance a trade deficit with foreign countries as well. The divergence in relative imports and exports by source and destination, however, does lend support to the notion that trade barriers divert trading patterns in favor of Central Canadian suppliers. Giving money to others is obviously an unnecessary component of a policy designed to increase demand for local products — and one that reduces local welfare. However, if money transferred to others is used for purchases of donor products, the donor may consider this as marginally better than the case where the transfers are not spent on donor products. This is clearly reminiscent of the literature on tied versus untied foreign aid.

important implications for Atlantic Canadian trade flows. This section examines the extent to which trade barriers affect current trading patterns, and how changes in these barriers resulting from different constitutional arrangements could perturb these patterns.

The Canadian market possesses many barriers to free trade. Research on the cost of interprovincial barriers has improved with data availability, but this is still a subject of some disagreement.[8] These estimates are difficult to make, since details of accepted and rejected bids on contracts would be needed for an accurate measure of the costs of procurement bias, as well as detailed information about the types of contracts subject to local preference.[9] In any event, smaller provinces tend to bear more of the cost of protectionism than the larger provinces, which can exploit "optimal tariff"-type advantages.[10] Trade barriers within the Atlantic region fragment an already small market even further, imposing relatively higher costs on provincial tax-

---

8 Frank Flatters and Richard Lipsey (*Common Ground for the Canadian Common Market* [Montreal: Institute for Research on Public Policy, 1983]) suggest that the present system of barriers is potentially quite damaging. Thomas Courchene (*Economic Management and the Division of Powers* [Toronto: University of Toronto Press, 1986]) states that the costs of a cure may be higher than that of the disease.

9 In 1991, the Canadian Manufacturers' Association (CMA) claimed that the cost of market barriers was $6 billion, of which $5 billion is attributed to inefficient procurement policies. See Canadian Manufacturers' Association, *Interprovincial Trade: Canada 1993, A Plan for the Creation of a Single Economic Market in Canada* (Toronto, 1991). An earlier study, however, suggests a range as low as $0.25–$2.5 billion in magnitude. See John Whalley, "Induced Distortions of Interprovincial Activity: An Overview of Issues," in Michael J. Trebilcock et al., eds., *Federation and the Canadian Economic Union* (Toronto: Ontario Economic Council, 1983). The differences between the Whalley estimates and those of the CMA would obviously appear far less dramatic if corrected for inflation.

In a 1977 study, Carl Shoup says that nontariff barriers to trade may be more important than procurement bias. See Carl Shoup, "Interregional Economic Barriers: The Canadian Provinces," in Ontario Economic Council, *Issues and Alternatives 1977: Intergovernmental Relations* (Toronto, 1977). Nontariff barriers are, however, particularly difficult to measure. Procurement bias may be less important than frequently imagined, according to a study by R.P. McAfee and J. McMillan, *Incentives in Government Contracting* (Toronto: Ontario Economic Council and the University of Toronto Press, 1988).

10 As pointed out in W. Milne, *Interprovincial Trade Barriers: A Survey and Assessment* (Toronto: Purchasing Management Association of Canada, 1987), p. 5.

payers for the privilege of using local producers. Other notable provincial trade barriers include brewing and liquor pricing policies, agricultural marketing boards, transportation regulation, and the licensing of professionals and corporations.[11]

While the three Maritime provinces have recently begun an experiment to reduce certain types of discriminatory practices, provincially determined barriers may not represent a serious distortion to the regional economy, although different sectors of society will not be uniformly affected.[12] It remains to be seen whether the Atlantic premiers will pursue these gains in the face of opposition from brewery workers, trucking operators, and local suppliers.

Provincially determined barriers are by no means the only source of inefficiency. One study suggests that some federal policies, such as the auto pact and freight rates, may be the most important sources of interregional distortions.[13] The *Maritime Freight Rates Act* and *Atlantic Region Freight Assistance Act* provided a 20–30 percent subsidy on rail freight within the region or to the rest of Canada. Other subsidies on truck, marine, and air freight pay up to 50 percent of the cost of transporting some commodities for the Atlantic portion of their

---

11 For more exhaustive lists of trade barriers, see, for example, Judith Maxwell and Caroline Pestieau, *Economic Realities of Contemporary Confederation*, Accent Québec 14 (Montreal: C.D. Howe Research Institute, 1980); Larry Grossman, *Interprovincial Economic Co-operation: Towards the Development of a Canadian Common Market* (Toronto: Ontario Ministry of Tourism, 1981); and Council of Maritime Premiers, *Challenge and Opportunity: A Discussion Paper on Maritime Premiers, Challenge and Opportunity: A Discussion Paper on Maritime Economic Integration* (Halifax, 1991).

12 One study indicates that the gains to Atlantic Canada from removing discriminatory liquor, trucking, and procurement policies would only amount to about $20 million. See Kenneth Norrie, Richard Simeon, and M. Krasnick, *Federalism and the Economic Union in Canada*, Collected Research Studies of the Royal Commission on the Economic Union and Development Prospects for Canada 59 (Toronto: University of Toronto Press, 1986).

13 See Fernand Martin, "Regional Impact of Selected Non-Expenditures Decisions of the Federal Government of Canada," in Queen's University, Institute for Intergovernmental Relations, *Proceedings of the Workshop on the Political Economy of Confederation, Kingston, Ont., November 8–10, 1978* (Kingston, Ont.: Queen's University, Institute for Intergovernmental Relations and the Economic Council of Canada, 1979).

journey.[14] These enormous subsidies have not only generated higher profits for Atlantic producers; they have also allowed inefficient firms to maintain operations that would otherwise have been terminated.

On the other hand, the international tariff structure has been cited as benefiting Ontario and Quebec at the expense of other regions.[15] Tariffs have distorted past decisions on the location of production facilities, possibly to the detriment of Atlantic Canada. However, many important Atlantic producers — such as fish processors — have enjoyed high rates of effective protection from national tariffs. For some of the producers who have remained in the area, tariffs have afforded an opportunity to remain in operation that may not otherwise have been available.

Future trading patterns likely will move in one of two opposite directions: toward greater integration if Canada remains whole, or toward increased fragmentation if Quebec separates. The Allaire Report of the Quebec Liberal Party identifies interprovincial trade barriers as impediments to constitutional development that should be removed.[16] Initiatives favoring reduced interprovincial barriers have also arisen in Western Canada and in the Maritime provinces. The support expressed for the removal of trade barriers should ensure this action if Canada remains whole. Although Quebec's vision of Canada calls for greater decentralization, Tom Courchene rejects the implication that this will necessarily mean greater market balkanization.[17]

Constitutional reform may require more serious policy changes at the federal level. If the movements toward greater decentralization, reduced federal expenditures, or greater economic efficiency of central government policies carry their current momentum into

---

14 R. Haack, D. Hughes, and R. Shapiro, *The Splintered Market: Barriers to Interprovincial Trade in Canadian Agriculture* (Toronto: James Lorimer, 1981), p. 2.

15 For an excellent background discussion, see Norrie, Simeon, and Krasnick, *Federalism and the Economic Union in Canada.*

16 Quebec Liberal Party, Constitutional Committee, *A Quebec Free to Choose* (Quebec, January 28, 1991), usually referred to as the "Allaire Report" after the Committee's Chairman, Jean Allaire.

17 See Thomas J. Courchene, "Analytical Perspectives on the Canadian Economic Union, " in Trebilcock et al., *Federalism and the Canadian Economic Union,* pp. 81–84.

practise, Atlantic Canadian business and freight subsidies may disappear. While the subsidies may be unnecessary to make some sectors of Atlantic Canada competitive, others may rely critically on subsidies to ensure their existence.

Increased international economic integration will also affect Atlantic Canada as trade barriers become increasingly subject to international agreements. Canada's involvement in the General Agreement on Tariffs and Trade, the Canada-U.S. Free Trade Agreement (FTA), and the proposed North American Free Trade Agreement indicates a growing commitment to free international markets. Although, historically, tariffs have been seen as having benefited Central Canada at the expense of the West and East, there is no reason to assume that movement toward a free trade system will do the opposite. Central Canada may have already captured the benefits of protection by having developed the most diversified and sophisticated manufacturing sector — at the expense of the other regions of Canada. Atlantic Canada clearly would not be immune to the removal of the tariff and nontariff barriers that offer significant effective protection to some of its important producers. Furthermore, the removal of protection for Central Canadian industries is more likely to result in the drift of production facilities to the United States rather than to the Atlantic provinces.

The major benefit of freer international trade will be lower prices — at the expense, however, of lost employment. Workers will be forced either to migrate or to accept lower wages. It is safe to predict that freer international trade will, in the short run, hurt Atlantic Canada, as protected industries become exposed and since new industries are slower to take advantage of any regional opportunities.[18]

On the other side of the constitutional coin is the possibility of Quebec separation, or of national dissolution. Quebec separation would probably reduce the urgency of decentralization for the rest of Canada, but there would still be the psychological blow to unity

18 Since economic adjustment always imposes some costs, this observation should not be misconstrued as an argument against free trade. Delaying freer trade may simply make future adjustment even worse, and avoiding international competition altogether may condemn an economy to permanent inefficiency.

of Atlantic Canada being physically disconnected from Ontario and the West. If the psychological disconnection leads to the elimination of transfers and subsidies, Atlantic Canada would be no better off than if it had accommodated Quebec's decentralist views.

The physical dislocation caused by an independent Quebec also engenders the possibility of trade disruption. Although Quebec studies have expressed desires to maintain membership in the FTA, such an unhindered trading relationship is by no means guaranteed.[19] The presence of an additional national boundary between Atlantic Canada and some of its markets may well prove to be more than just a nominal inconvenience. Boundary questions may also arise about the Labrador-Quebec border, coastal boundaries between Quebec and its Atlantic neighbors, and the status of northern Quebec, whose aboriginal inhabitants may well object to their separation from the rest of Canada.[20] While friendly cooperation in settling these boundary questions would be desirable, the process of resolution may well include trade disruptions as a negotiating tactic. Newfoundland's exports and potential exports of hydro-electricity and minerals, which currently pass through Quebec, are an example of some trade flows that could be vulnerable to interference. Noncooperation could also complicate the exploitation of hydro-electric potential in Labrador.

In short, the current pattern of Atlantic Canadian trade reflects the presence of both provincially and federally determined barriers.

---

19 For a decidedly optimistic discussion of Quebec's access to external markets if separation occurs, see Ivan Bernier, "Le maintien de l'accès aux marchés extérieurs: certaines questions juridiques soulevées dans l'hypothèse de la souveraineté du Québec"; and Secrétariat de la Commission sur l'avenir politique et constitutionnel du Québec [Bélanger-Campeau Secretariat], "L'accès du Québec aux marchés extérieurs et à l'espace économique canadien," both in Quebec, Commission on the Political and Constitutional Future of Quebec [Bélanger-Campeau Commission]. *Éléments d'analyse économique pertinents à la révision du statut politique et constitutionnel du Québec* [Background papers], vol. 1 (Quebec, 1991). It should be noted that if the Bélanger-Campeau Report's optimistic view should prove unfounded for Quebec, it may well prove untrue — at least in part — for the other provinces, even if they remain united.

20 Under the worst scenario of complete dissolution, the boundary complications may be exacerbated by territorial disputes among the Atlantic provinces themselves!

It appears that the current constitutional mood favors the removal of transportation subsidies and other barriers. Hence, the policies that benefit Atlantic Canada are more likely to be on the constitutional chopping block than those that may damage the region. In addition, the potential for new territorial jurisdictions introduces added uncertainty for the region, since the most likely change — an independent Quebec — is geographically connected to Atlantic Canada.

The Scope for Adjustment

In the absence of substantial transfers from the rest of Canada, the current trading structure of Atlantic Canada would be unsustainable. The current volume of imports — and hence a significant component of regional living standards — could only be maintained with a dramatic increase in exports or a substantial capital account surplus. These two routes for import finance will be considered in turn.

Improved export performance is generally achieved through relative price adjustments caused by currency depreciation, domestic price and wage deflation, or productivity increases that induce cost reductions. Increased exports are also produced through favorable external demand conditions, the presence of which are largely independent of any locally determined policies.

Currency depreciation should improve the balance of payments in the long run, although the short-run dynamics are extremely sensitive to elasticities in traded goods markets. There is an extensive literature on exchange-rate adjustment within the context of less-developed countries, and considerable controversy about the effectiveness of currency devaluation as a key component of structural adjustment programs.[21] Currency manipulation, however, is clearly unavailable to provinces or regions within Canada, and even the most decentralizing proposals in the Bélanger-Campeau or Allaire reports favor a common Canadian currency. It is only under the most extreme circumstances of dissolution that the Atlantic prov-

---

21 For an excellent presentation of the topic, see S. Edwards, *Real Exchange Rates, Devaluation, and Adjustment* (Cambridge, Mass.: MIT Press, 1989).

inces can individually or collectively use an exchange-rate policy to improve their regional balance of payments.

Wage and price adjustments may also assist in structural adjustment. As a small open economy, Atlantic Canada is unlikely to have any influence on real international prices for traded goods. Atlantic Canadian prices will also be tied even more closely to Canadian prices due to the presence of "national" producers and retailers. Wage adjustment may also be constrained by the presence of national labor markets and policies. As with currency manipulation, it may only be under circumstances of severe constitutional dislocation that Atlantic Canadian labor markets may be able to separate sufficiently from the Canadian labor market to permit substantial wage flexibility. Finally, reductions in regional wages are likely to result in the emigration of the most skilled and productive workers.[22]

Currency and wage changes that improve the balance of payments work in two ways: they improve trade performance by shifting relative prices, and they inhibit imports by reducing living standards. These policies, therefore, would merely adjust Atlantic Canadians to lower living standards; they would not permit Atlantic Canada to sustain its current level of imports. Improvements in productivity and output, however, can improve living standards, and productivity improvements in the traded goods sector can compensate for or finance the current level of imports.

Improved productivity is generally considered "good", since it should always lead to greater availability of goods and services in an economy.[23] It should be noted, however, that in Atlantic Canada some disturbing distribution problems may arise from productivity improvements. The exporting sector in Atlantic Canada is dominated by resource extractors and processors. While there are some notable exceptions in the services and manufacturing sectors, the

---

22 Any discussion of wages and labor markets will obviously depend on migration conditions. Migration as a form of regional adjustment is discussed later in the essay.

23 There are, of course, some model configurations that can generate unfavorable results in the presence of trade distortions.

bulk of Atlantic Canadian employment, output, and trade in the goods-producing sectors depends on the exploitation of forests, minerals, agriculture, and the fisheries. We believe that in sectors with resources that are either nonrenewable or "fixed" in the sense of having a very low elasticity of supply, improved labor productivity will lead to displaced workers without increasing net production. Hence, productivity increases in Atlantic Canada may be unable either to improve export performance for the region or to increase living standards without the emigration of the unemployed. The typical assumption in economics that displaced workers will move on to other activities is the crux of the Keynesian-versus-Classical debate. Atlantic Canada seems to be unblushingly Keynesian. The region typically tolerates abnormally high rates of unemployment, and there are few sectors that seem capable of any substantive absorption of labor.[24] Although the long run may include the development of a competitive manufacturing sector capable of employing the Atlantic Canadian labor force, past experience suggests that such industrial development is difficult to induce, even with substantial amounts of federal money.[25]

The present current account deficit of Atlantic Canada is financed primarily with a capital account surplus based on transfer payments from the rest of Canada. Constitutional reforms that reduce transfer payments[26] will obviously restrict Atlantic Canada's

---

24 It is unlikely that unemployment in the region is truly "Keynesian" in the sense of being due to cyclical deficiencies in aggregate demand. The presence of unemployment insurance and other personal transfers has contributed to the presence of high rates of unemployment in the region.

25 Optimism about long-run prospects would do little for displaced workers concerned about the short run. To paraphrase Keynes, in the long run we are all residing in Mississauga.

26 Transfer payments are discussed in detail below. All the signals would suggest that transfer payments will be reduced. The governments of Alberta and British Columbia have often stated their displeasure at having to finance Confederation. Quebec — itself a net recipient of transfers according to most studies — has also produced reports that favor reductions of transfer payments, and certainly a reorientation of transfers towards infrastructure development and other production incentives. The Allaire Report is one such example.

capacity to import. However, capital account surpluses can also be generated by investment flows and borrowing, which could theoretically replace transfers as the method of financing current Atlantic Canadian living standards.

Net investment flow data for the provinces were not available for this study. In any case, it is unlikely that new investment flows would be able to replace federal transfer payments. Atlantic Canada is highly dependent on the federal government for expenditures and transfers;[27] any redefinition of that relationship is likely to cause greater uncertainty, at least in the short run. Uncertainty will tend to discourage, not encourage, additional investment. Constitutional reforms that strengthen the Canadian economic union by reducing internal trade barriers may induce some investment in the region if local manufacturers could exploit economies of scale, but the effect will probably be small. Further investment in the resource sectors is unlikely, given current capacity and resource limitations, and non-mobile physical capital is likely to be in relative abundance if there is any reduction in economic activity brought on by the withdrawal of any federal activities. Finally, there is the possibility of creating a regional scheme to direct local savings into the regional economy, as Quebec has done. The theoretical support for such a program is weak, however, and could only be justified in the presence of demonstrated market failure.[28] In order for such a program to improve the regional capital account, it would have to reverse net capital flows out of the region. However, the larger the net outflows prevented by such a program, the larger the market distortion. The likely results of such a policy are simply lower returns on savings. The artificial isolation of the capital market may also reduce opportunities for risk diversifica-

---

27 Federal expenditures and transfers represented 33 percent of final domestic demand for the Atlantic provinces in 1989. The equivalent measure for the other provinces was 20.6 percent (see Statistics Canada, *Fixed Capital Flows and Stocks*, Cat. no. 13-211).

28 Imperfect information is a likely candidate as a cause of market failure. It is not clear, however, that a regional investment program would have any advantage over present financial institutions in identifying appropriate investment opportunities.

tion. Finally, previous investment programs in the Atlantic region seem to have been unable to perform as well as have Quebec's.

A capital account surplus generated by government borrowing seems even less likely than private investment flows. Even in the absence of constitutional uncertainty, Atlantic Canadian provinces seem to be at or near their credit ceilings. New Brunswick has the best bond ratings in Atlantic Canada, but even these are low by Canadian standards. Furthermore, interest-rate spreads tend to be even less favorable for the Atlantic provinces than the bond ratings suggest.[29] All four provinces are close to the critical cusp between A and B ratings (Newfoundland having already fallen below A by some standards), where investment by many institutional lenders becomes unavailable and where even unconstrained investors are wary. Any diminution of the strong links between the federal government and the Atlantic provinces would presumably make borrowing by the provincial governments even harder, since lenders presently evaluate Atlantic Canada's ability to pay within the context of probable federal intervention in the case of repayment difficulties. In the extreme case of dissolution, Atlantic Canada may be faced with the prospect of capital flight caused by increased uncertainty, and perhaps even the possibility of currency risk. Provincial government budgets have highlighted the absence of any substantial borrowing capacity; following the most recent Newfoundland budget, ministers cited pressure from financial markets as a critical determinant of the restrictions placed on expenditures.

In conclusion, Atlantic Canada is highly sensitive to federal government transfers and expenditures. The current trend in the

---

29 Bond ratings were acquired for June 12, 1991, on long-term issues. The rating services examined were Moody's, Standard and Poor's, the Dominion Bond Rating Service, and the Canadian Bond Rating Service. According to these ratings, New Brunswick and Manitoba were fairly equal and ahead of Saskatchewan and Nova Scotia, which were also close in the ratings. Prince Edward Island (despite its relatively low public-sector debt ratios) was rated second-lowest in Canada, ahead of last-place Newfoundland, which three of the four services rated below the A gradings. We acknowledge the kind assistance of Mr. J. Rudd of RBC Dominion Securities Inc. for data and discussion.

constitutional debate seems to be towards decentralization, with reduced federal activity. Even centralists seem to have accepted the need for reform and reduced federal expenditures, if only to address the current budget deficit. The impact of federal expenditure and transfer changes will depend crucially on the speed and dimension of any reductions. Atlantic Canada does not appear to have the means to provide short-run substitutes for federal funds if these should be reduced quickly, making the process of adjustment to long-run equilibrium unusually painful. Furthermore, the absence of flexibility inherent in a resource-based economy suggests that the Atlantic region is unlikely to be able to rebound from any recession induced by federal expenditure reductions.

Transfers

There have been concerns over regional disparities since the birth of Canada as a nation. Initially, these concerns centered around the inability of the governments of the poorer provinces to provide the same level of services to their citizens as could the governments of the wealthier provinces. For example, at the time of Confederation New Brunswick received "a special 10 year grant in recognition of its unique financial needs, and the same provision was extended to Nova Scotia in 1869."[30] This arrangement gives credence to the notion of fiscal balance and the redistributive role of the federal government through transfers to the provinces. More recently, in 1948, Term 29 of the Terms of Union between Newfoundland and Canada guaranteed that the level of public services offered in that province would be at a level comparable to the other Atlantic provinces.

The crude notions of fiscal equity that existed in the earlier years of Confederation eventually gave way to more sophisticated con-

---

30 Kenneth Norrie, Robin Boadway, and Lars Osberg, "The Constitution and the Social Contract" (Paper presented at the conference, "The Economic Dimensions of Constitutional Change," sponsored by the John Deutsch Institute for the Study of Economic Policy, Kingston, Ont., June 4–6, 1991, Mimeographed), p. 3.

cepts that were reflected in the emerging transfer structure.[31] For example, grants such as Established Programs Financing (EPF) designed to achieve national levels of service have helped to achieve vertical fiscal balance.[32] By way of contrast, equalization payments are designed to provide for horizontal fiscal balance — that is, "to equalize the capacity of provincial governments to provide certain levels of public services."[33] Some conditional grants may even be regarded as a means of dealing with specific externalities between jurisdictions.[34]

The concept of national equity or the national social contract has much wider dimensions than just the transfer of funds from the federal to the provincial level of government. The federal government on its own or in cooperation with the provinces transfers income to individuals in order to promote a more equitable distribution of society's resources. The federal personal income tax system can be used to promote equity, and with the most recent reforms has become a much more important instrument for achieving this social objective.[35] However, family allowances, old age pensions, and unemployment insurance (UI) are the three most important federal transfer programs to individuals.

Transfers to business can generally be thought of as an attempt to promote interregional equity by promoting the creation of job opportunities for individuals in the regions in which they like to live.

31 For a much more thorough discussion of the issues, see Richard M. Bird, "Federal-Provincial Fiscal Arrangements: Is There an Agenda for the 1990s?" in Ronald L. Watts and Douglas M. Brown, eds., *Canada: The State of the Federation, 1990* (Kingston, Ont.: Queen's University, Institute of Intergovernmental Relations, 1990), pp. 109–136.

32 Norrie, Boadway, and Osberg ("The Constitution and the Social Contract," p. 2) state that the EPF grants reflect "a commitment to individual equity on the basis of national citizenship."

33 Bird, "Federal-Provincial Fiscal Arrangements," p. 113.

34 An obvious example is in postsecondary education, where one province may subsidize the education of an individual who may subsequently move to another province.

35 This is especially true given the introduction of refundable tax credits.

Section 36 of the Canadian Constitution

36. (1) Without altering the legislative authority of Parliament or of the provincial legislatures, or the rights of any of them with respect to the exercise of their legislative authority, Parliament and the legislatures, together with the government of Canada and the provincial governments are committed to
    (a) promoting equal opportunities for the well-being of Canadians;
    (b) furthering economic development to reduce disparity in opportunities;
and providing essential public services of reasonable quality to all Canadians.

(2) Parliament and the government of Canada are committed to the principle of making equalization payments to ensure that provincial governments have sufficient revenues to provide reasonably comparable levels of public services at reasonably comparable levels of taxation.

A commitment to this form of equity is contained in Section 36.1 of the *Constitution Act of 1982* (see the box above).

Finally, the federal government may effect a transfer by providing goods and services to a province at levels above which it could provide itself. The difficulty with this concept is that these services themselves may involve externalities that are interprovincial in nature: naval defense expenditures made in Halifax may benefit all of Canada rather than one particular province.

Figures 1 and 2 provide different perspectives for looking at the types of transfers to Atlantic Canada. Figure 1 shows federal government expenditures for the region by type of expenditure in constant dollar per capita terms. While federal government expenditures on final goods and services seem to be declining slightly, it is too early to state if there are trends in the other expenditures on a real per capita basis. The pattern for the Atlantic region is markedly different than for Canada as a whole: for Canada, real per capita grants have been declining since 1985. Figure 2 relates these per capita expenditures to the Canadian average. In all categories, the ratio is greater than 1.0 and has remained relatively constant; the exception is transfers to business, which seem to have fallen and now approach the national average.

A crude approximation of the overall relative importance of net federal inflows can be found by examining federal government

Figure 1: *Per Capita Federal Government Transfers to, and Expenditures in, Atlantic Canada, 1971–89*

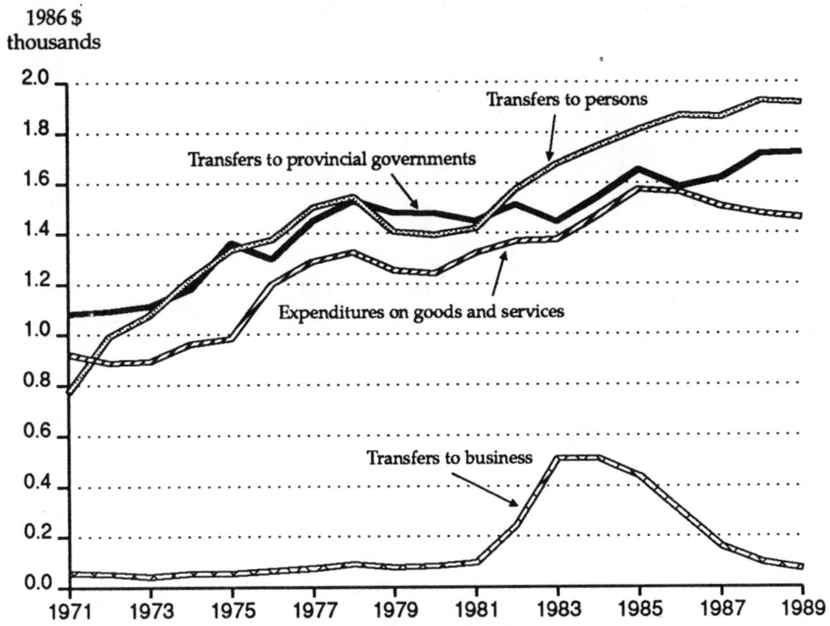

Sources: Statistics Canada, *Provincial Economic Accounts, Annual Estimates*, Cat. no. 13-213; idem, *Postcensal Annual Estimates of Population by Marital Status, Age, Sex and Components of Growth for Canada, Provinces and Territories*, Cat. no. 91-210.

savings by province as a percentage of final domestic demand. This measure provides an estimate of the percentage of domestic expenditures financed by net federal cash inflows.[36] For the Atlantic provinces, these data are shown in Figure 3.

This figure clearly shows the trend toward a growing dependency on federal cash flows for the Atlantic provinces from 1961 to 1985. Since 1985, however, dependency seems to exhibit a downward trend. Given current federal government policies of deficit control and reduced transfers to the provinces, there is every reason to believe that this trend will continue.

36 This measure assumes that all of the cash inflows are spent and none is saved. While this is true for expenditures that represent transfers to other levels of government or to businesses, it is not true of transfers to individuals.

Figure 2: *Federal Government Transfers to, and Expenditures In, Atlantic Canada as an Index of the Canadian Average, 1971–89*

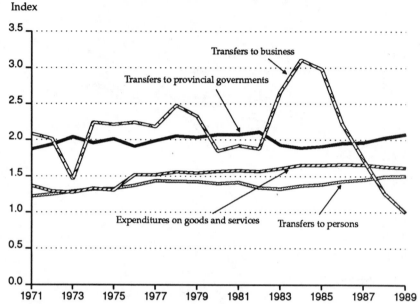

Sources: Statistics Canada, *Provincial Economic Accounts, Annual Estimates*, Cat. no. 13-213; idem, *Postcensal Annual Estimates of Population by Marital Status, Age, Sex and Components of Growth for Canada, Provinces and Territories*, Cat. no. 91-210.

Figure 3 indicates that Prince Edward Island has maintained its position as the Atlantic province most dependent on federal funds. The experiences of Nova Scotia and Newfoundland have diverged, with dependence decreasing in the former and increasing in the latter. Part of the reason that Atlantic Canada's dependency has fallen relative to the rest of the country is that federal government savings in the region have stabilized, while domestic demand grew from 1985 to 1989.

In 1978, Tom Courchene wrote that "the transfer system plays a major role in providing the net inflow of dollars that the Maritimes needs to maintain its net deficit on interregional trade," and that it "allows their consumption levels to be greater than would be the case

Figure 3: ***Federal Government Savings as a Percentage of Final Domestic Demand, Atlantic Provinces and Canada, 1961–89***

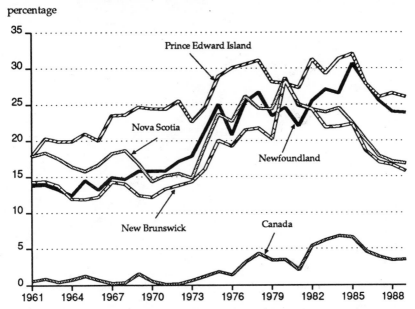

Source: Statistics Canada, *Provincial Economic Accounts, Annual Estimates*, Cat. no. 13-213.

in the absence of such transfers."[37] In Figure 4, we trace out net federal savings and net exports for the region for the 1961–89 period. The results from simple linear regressions using net exports as the dependent variable support the contention that federal savings explain much of the variation in provincial net imports. The weakest results are shown for New Brunswick.[38] We note that traditionally there is a relatively heavier dependence on federal funds in Prince Edward Island and Newfoundland than in New Brunswick and

---

37 Thomas J. Courchene, "Avenues of Adjustment: The Transfer System and Regional Disparities," in *Canadian Confederation at the Crossroads* (Vancouver: Fraser Institute, 1978), p. 152.

38 The adjusted R^2 for the regression is 0.98145. Stronger results might have been obtained if there were not data problems associated with net imports, which, in the *Provincial Economic Accounts*, also includes the residual error of estimate.

Figure 4:   *Federal Government Savings In, and Net Exports to, Atlantic Canada, 1961–89*

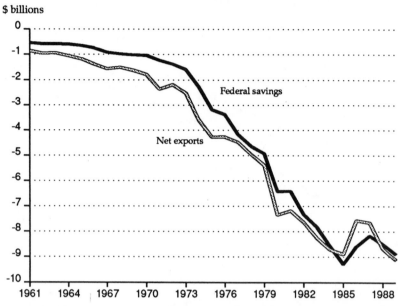

Source: Statistics Canada, *Provincial Economic Accounts, Annual Estimates*, Cat. no. 13-213.

Nova Scotia.[39] These results provide strong support for Courchene's observations.

In the following subsections, we examine the historical pattern of federal transfers to governments, businesses, and individuals by type of transfer. The simulation results presented in the last section include modifications of some or all of these transfer programs.

Transfers to Government

As noted above, transfers to the provincial governments have permitted the Atlantic provinces to provide a reasonable level of public

---

39 It should be noted that the level of dependence in these last two provinces is still much greater than that of Quebec. The federal government dissaves in every province except Alberta and Ontario. In order to do this, it must run a deficit and borrow funds.

services without an unreasonable tax effort. Transfers have also helped these provinces to maintain national standards, particularly in health care and postsecondary education.[40] Indeed, Section 36 of the *Constitution Act of 1982* virtually guarantees transfers to the provinces to facilitate the provision of public services and the promotion of equal opportunities.[41]

Because the fiscal capacities of the Atlantic provinces are among the lowest in the country, transfers from the federal government are particularly important. Figure 5 demonstrates the relative importance of federal government transfers to the provinces by showing these transfers as a percentage of total provincial revenues. This figure illustrates that the dependence on federal transfers to the provincial governments has been declining in recent years, yet remains high. In 1989, Prince Edward Island and Newfoundland received about 46 percent of their revenue from the federal government, while New Brunswick and Nova Scotia each received about 39 percent. These percentages were well above all of the other provinces; Manitoba is ranked fifth at almost 29 percent.

There are three main categories of transfers to the provincial governments: equalization payments, EPF (cash),[42] and conditional/shared cost grants. Figure 6 provides the relative breakdown of each of these categories for fiscal year 1990/91. In each of the provinces, equalization payments are by far the most important source of cash transfers from the federal government, and their

---

40 See, for example, Robin Boadway and Frank Flatters, "Federal-Provincial Fiscal Relations Revisited: Some Consequences of Recent Constitutional and Policy Developments," in Melville McMillan, ed., *Provincial Public Finances*, vol. 2, *Plaudits, Problems, and Prospects* (Toronto: Canadian Tax Foundation, 1991).

41 The exact interpretation of the clauses under Section 36 awaits rulings by the courts. The fact that Quebec has not ratified the Constitution suggests that Section 36 and the principles behind it may be far from universally accepted. Indeed, the Allaire Report calls for a new equalization formula and a movement away from national standards that promote centralist tendencies.

42 In the *Provincial Economic Accounts*, it seems as though at least some of the tax transfers associated with EPF were included in "miscellaneous", which is Line 18, Table 15 of these accounts.

Figure 5:   *Federal Transfers to Provincial Governments in Atlantic Canada as a Percentage of Their Total Revenue, 1961–89*

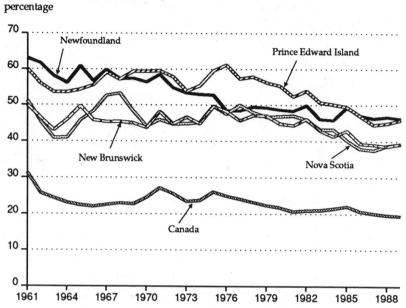

Source: Statistics Canada, *Provincial Economic Accounts, Annual Estimates*, Cat. no. 13-213.

importance relative to the cash transfer portion of EPF has been increasing. Equalization payments in three of the provinces — New Brunswick, Nova Scotia, and Newfoundland — exceed $900 million a year. In contrast, EPF cash transfers have remained almost stagnant since 1984/85; in all four provinces, the dollar amount of the EPF transfers was slightly greater in 1986/87 than in 1990/91. Shared-cost programs, of which the most important is the Canada Assistance Program (CAP), have also been growing in importance.

Federal government transfers should bring each province to the position where it is possible to provide public services at reasonable levels without an undue burden on its taxpayers. By and large, this has been accomplished, and the spirit of Section 36(2) of the *Constitution Act* seems to have been met. Table 1 demonstrates that while, in 1987/88, provincial-local own-source revenue was well below the

Figure 6:   *Federal Transfers to Provincial Governments in Atlantic Canada by Category, fiscal year 1990/91*

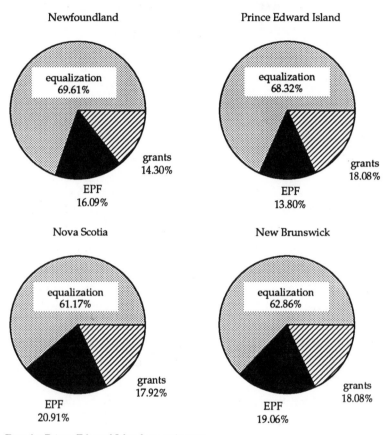

Newfoundland

equalization
69.61%

grants
14.30%

EPF
16.09%

Prince Edward Island

equalization
68.32%

grants
18.08%

EPF
13.80%

Nova Scotia

equalization
61.17%

grants
17.92%

EPF
20.91%

New Brunswick

equalization
62.86%

grants
18.08%

EPF
19.06%

Note: Data for Prince Edward Island are estimates.

Sources: Governments of Newfoundland and Labrador; Nova Scotia; and New Brunswick.

national average, federal transfers in all cases brought the Atlantic provinces almost to the average.

EPF grants, although they are now unconditional, were conditional until 1977. A good case could be made to restore the conditionality of EPF on the grounds that these grants are used to provide essential services such as health care and postsecondary education at national levels. In addition, the emigration of a large number of

**Table 1:   *Indices of Fiscal Capacity in the
Provincial and Local Sectors, fiscal year 1987/88***
(as a percentage of the national average)

	Without Transfers	With Transfers
Newfoundland	61%	96%
Prince Edward Island	65	96
Nova Scotia	76	94
New Brunswick	71	96

Source: Melville McMillan, "Introduction," in Melville McMillan, ed., *Provincial Public Finances*, vol. 1, *Plaudits, Problems, and Prospects* (Toronto: Canadian Tax Foundation, 1991), Table 1.1

individuals with postsecondary education from the Atlantic region represents spillovers that are not recovered. The stated objective of the federal government to reduce the EPF cash transfers may serve to increase the level of economic inefficiency by failing to recognize these externalities. Ideally, EPF grants should be conditional, and the level of the grants should reflect the degree of externalities present.

CAP grants are conditional matching grants. A difficulty with this grant structure, and an irony with this particular program, is that although the program is designed to help provinces meet national standards, the poorer provinces simply do not have the fiscal capacity to do so. The implication is that, in the poorer Atlantic provinces, the plan is less successful in bringing families towards the low-income cut off levels than in the richer provinces.

While the importance of federal government transfers to the Atlantic provinces as a percentage of total revenue has been diminishing, there can be no dispute that without such transfers the provincial governments in the region could not provide the same level of public service.

Will these federal transfers survive constitutional reform? Some economists[43] have argued that transfers are guaranteed under the *Constitution Act*. Section 36(1) can be used to justify expenditures

43 Most notably, Boadway and Flatters, "Federal-Provincial Fiscal Relations Revisited."

funded by EPF and CAP, while Section 36(2) guarantees equalization payments. Quebec has not signed the *Constitution Act of 1982* and seems to disagree with these transfer provisions, if one is to use the Allaire Report as an indicator. For example, the Report states:

> It is becoming increasingly obvious that the Canadian federal state is based on centralizing practices dictated by an inflexible will to standardize public services to the utmost and the pursuit of the so-called "national policies".[44]

As part of the solution, the report recommends that

> Equalization must be changed to place greater emphasis on improving the conditions of production in the recipient regions. The focus of the support provided will shift from maintaining public services of comparable quality to investment assistance in physical infrastructures, communications, transportation, etc.[45]

Clearly, the Allaire Report and the Constitution offer fundamentally different interpretations regarding the need for and the purpose of transfers. Part of the concern expressed by Newfoundland Premier Clyde Wells revolves around the implementation of Section 36 and the need for provincial governments to have the financial capability to provide national levels of service. Indeed, Term 29 of the Terms of Union between Newfoundland and Canada guarantees that the province will have the financial capability to provide a level of service (if the province wishes to) comparable to that provided in the Maritime provinces. It is difficult to imagine how equalization payments could be changed in the manner suggested by the Allaire Report without violating the spirit of the Constitution as it is perceived in Atlantic Canada.

We strongly suspect that transfers from the federal to the provincial governments will become the critical focus for the constitutional debate. These transfers are not only the battleground for the

44 Allaire Report, p. 4.
45 Ibid., p. 40.

intergovernmental turf war over the division of powers; they may
also be perceived as the only means of providing relief to those
regions that are harmed by any changes in transfers to business and
individuals. Hence, the provincial governments in Atlantic Canada
may accept that efficiency and intraprovincial equity may require
alterations that reduce the amount of unemployment insurance
benefits flowing into the region, but only if it is compensated with
additional transfers to the provincial governments. Such an accommodation may satisfy Quebec's decentralist aspirations, but it is
likely to run into opposition in both Quebec and the rest of Canada
for fiscal reasons.

Transfers to Business

The rationale for federal transfers to business might be found in
Section 36(1) of the Constitution, which commits the federal government and the provincial governments to encourage economic development "to reduce the disparity in opportunities." The Atlantic
provinces would clearly see many of the transfers to business in this
perspective, a view emphasizing equity rather than efficiency. Many
economists and organizations, including the federal Department of
Finance, have argued that such transfers have not reduced disparities by changing the existing economic structure.[46] Casual empirical
evidence would tend to support these conclusions: earned income
in the Atlantic provinces as a percentage of personal income has not
increased markedly over the past 30 years, and earned real income
per capita indexed to the national average has increased only slightly
for three of the four Atlantic provinces. Prince Edward Island is an
exception.

It is clear from Figures 1 and 2 that federal transfers to the region
on a constant dollar per capita basis have been declining in recent

---

[46] In its Twenty-Seventh Annual Review, the Economic Council of Canada adopts
a similar position. See *Financing Confederation: Today and Tomorrow* (Ottawa:
Supply and Services Canada, 1982), p. 49.

years, and although these grant levels are historically above the Canadian average, they did drop below this average in 1987. The large grant increases in the 1980s[47] were associated with the Petroleum Incentive Program (PIP), which was responsible for a great deal of oil and gas exploration off the east coast. It should be noted that Hibernia was discovered before the PIP program was in place. In addition, in 1974 subsidies were paid to the importers of crude oil in order to shield consumers from the oil price shocks affecting the world economy. The subsidies affected those provinces east of Ontario and were quite substantial when their value peaked in 1981; the value of the subsidy to Nova Scotia was almost $743 million in 1981, while New Brunswick received $826 million in that same year.[48] If these grants to oil importers under the National Energy Program and PIP grants are removed (see Figure 7), then the subsidy pattern for Atlantic Canada is not that different from the national one, and grant levels approach the national average. These grants were $168 (constant 1986 dollars) per capita for the region in 1989, compared with $168 for Quebec and $176 for Ontario; the Prairie provinces receive much larger grants per capita because of agricultural subsidies. One might think of UI benefits to fishermen as a substitute for agricultural subsidies to farmers.[49]

In addition, it could be argued that a large portion of the subsidies and capital assistance to business has benefited corporations outside of the Atlantic region and has not served to increase the productive capacity and the opportunities available in the region.[50]

Any number of efficiency arguments exist for eliminating subsidies and capital assistance to business. While these programs might

---

47 Starting in 1982 and peaking in 1984, with $835 million being spent in the region.

48 In 1981, total subsidies under this program peaked at nearly $3.8 billion, with slightly over $2 billion going to Quebec.

49 The comparison really depends on the design features of particular programs, of which there are many.

50 For a discussion of the high rates of "leakage" from the Atlantic region toward Central Canada, see Maxwell and Pestieau, *Economic Realities of Contemporary Confederation*.

Figure 7:   *Per Capita Federal Government Assistance to Business in Atlantic Canada, 1971–89*

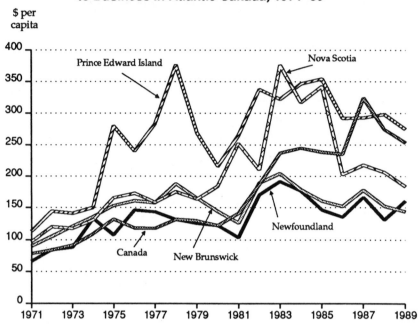

Note: Excludes energy components.

Sources: Statistics Canada, *Provincial Economic Accounts, Annual Estimates*, Cat. no. 13-213; idem, *Postcensal Annual Estimates of Population by Marital Status, Age, Sex and Components of Growth for Canada, Provinces and Territories*, Cat. no. 91-210.

increase regional efficiency if there were large economies of scale and/or scope present, there seems to be little evidence to validate this assumption. In the absence of documented market failures, the subsidies may simply be trade distorting and may increase production inefficiencies. There is also reason to believe that grants to individual firms may permit inefficient operators to force efficient firms out of business.

Although there may be an economic case for limited government subsidies, we doubt that the changes in relative prices brought about by the elimination of transfers to business would be serious for Atlantic Canada. The region may even benefit from the process of rationalization. Business transfers, however, also have an income effect, since the region is a net transfer recipient. Any changes in business transfer programs that are not compensated for in other transfers will therefore represent real income losses for the region and require adjustment. The Atlantic provinces are likely to resist reductions in business transfers due to the close relationship between business and government in the region, and because business subsidies result in employment opportunities that can be immediately attributed to the government. While this tendency may diminish as internationally competitive producers in the region add their voices to the call for freer trade, the bottom line for the provincial governments will still be the magnitude of net transfers to the region.

Transfers to Persons

In terms of net cash inflows into the region, transfers to persons are larger than any of the other expenditure categories.[51] Unlike the rest of Canada, these transfers to the Atlantic region have been growing in real per capita terms since 1985. Figure 8 provides a breakdown of the relative amounts spent on each of the transfer programs to individuals. Clearly, unemployment insurance is the most important, representing 43 percent of total transfers to individuals in 1989, followed by old age security payments. Figure 9 shows that UI benefits in constant dollars per capita have increased rapidly since 1971, in spite of a break in the pattern during the 1979–81 period. Newfoundlanders are the most dependent on UI payments in the region, while Nova Scotians are the least dependent. This difference in dependency can probably be explained by differences in access to full-year employment; many of those receiving UI benefits in Newfoundland live in rural areas and work in seasonal occupations. These benefits, when combined with employment income and household production, result in a standard of living that may be fairly close to families living in urban areas of the country employed in full-year jobs. In fact, the percentage of people who own their own homes is much higher in Newfoundland than in any other province.

---

51 This can easily be verified by examining Figure 1.

Figure 8: *Income Components as a Percentage of Total Federal Government Transfers to Persons in Atlantic Canada, 1961–89*

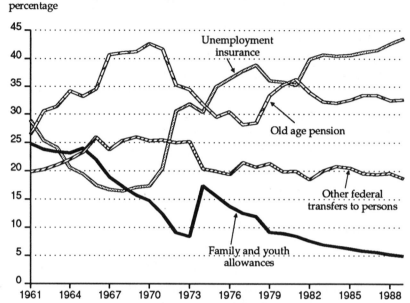

Sources: Statistics Canada, *Provincial Economic Accounts, Annual Estimates,* Cat. no. 13-213; idem, *Postcensal Annual Estimates of Population by Marital Status, Age, Sex and Components of Growth for Canada, Provinces and Territories,* Cat. no. 91-210.

However, many young people find this life less than ideal, since the dependency is well recognized and the possibility for improvement is limited.

In considering changes to the policy on transfers to persons, this paper will concentrate on changes to the UI program.[52] Recent changes, taking effect in 1990, make the program self-financing. There is continuing concern about dependency on the program, especially for Atlantic Canadians. Most policymakers and econo-

---

52 Changes in other major transfer programs are likely to be less dramatic. Programs associated with pensions are notoriously difficult to cut back, as the federal Progressive Conservative government learned with deindexation. These programs represent an intergenerational component of the social contract in which all life-cycle and permanent-income-type individuals have a stake. Changing intertemporal contracts appear to violate our notions of justice more than altering interregional agreements, perhaps with some justification.

Figure 9: *Per Capita Unemployment Insurance Benefits, Atlantic Canada, 1971–89*

1986 $
thousands

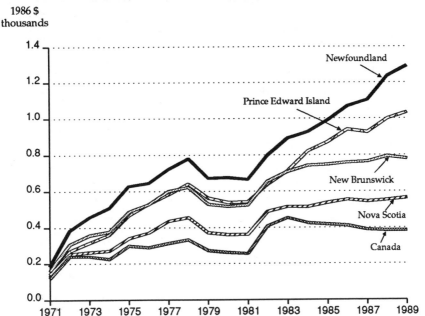

Sources: Statistics Canada, *Provincial Economic Accounts, Annual Estimates*, Cat. no. 13-213; idem, *Postcensal Annual Estimates of Population by Marital Status, Age, Sex and Components of Growth for Canada, Provinces and Territories*, Cat. no. 91-210.

mists would agree that the current program violates the principles of horizontal and vertical equity and reduces labor market efficiency by hindering the adjustment process without addressing the source of the problem. The program continues to exist in its present form despite calls for change because an acceptable income security program does not exist. The Allaire Report states that Quebec should be responsible for UI, along with vocational training and other labor-related policies. For the federal government, a UI program self-financed at the provincial level would avoid political problems and would be consistent with insurance-based principles.[53]

---

53 The present UI system is a combination of the principles of insurance and income security.

As with other transfers and subsidies, the UI program is a source of net financial injections into Atlantic Canada. The substitution effects of changes to these programs are likely to be tolerated, if not enjoyed, by Atlantic Canadians and their governments. The income effects generated by program changes will be less well received. To explore this question in more detail, the first simulation presented in the last section deals with changes to the UI program.

The programs that transfer income from wealthy regions and individuals to the less fortunate need to be made more efficient and less damaging to incentive structures. There seems to be an emerging consensus on the urgency of reform and the directions it should take. Therefore, the critical element of the constitutional debate for Atlantic Canadians will probably be about the level of net transfers, and not the form in which they are transmitted. The chances of a consensus in this area are remote. Ontario, Alberta, and British Columbia are unlikely to have either the will or the ability to maintain current levels of transfers, and governments in these provinces have already said as much. The economies of the Atlantic provinces are already under tremendous pressure to adjust; any reduction in transfers will be translated immediately and in full into higher out-migration and/or reduced living standards. Aspects of the migration adjustment process are discussed in the next section.

Migration Patterns

If a region experiences an unfavorable economic shock, labor mobility becomes the main avenue of adjustment when wage rates are linked either directly or indirectly to national or international labor markets and the provincial economies operate in a common currency area. The migration of labor is also determined by job availability; therefore, migration from Atlantic Canada would be generated by a lack of employment opportunity in this region coupled with employment opportunity elsewhere.

Census data from 1981 and 1986 show that the pattern of migration for the Atlantic provinces is similar to that of other provinces. Ontario and Quebec stand out as exceptions. For example, while 6.3 percent of Prince Edward Island's population moved out of the province in the 1981–86 period, only 1.79 percent of Quebec's did so. Other census data tend to confirm this result. Table 2 shows that in 1986, 91.9 percent of those born in Quebec were living there; the same figures for Nova Scotia and Saskatchewan were 74.6 percent and 60.2 percent, respectively.

To where did people from the Atlantic provinces migrate? Table 3 provides some answers for the 1981–86 period. Ontario was the favorite destination for all Atlantic Canadian emigrants, with Nova Scotia as the next favorite destination for migrants from the other Atlantic provinces.

The evidence on migration patterns provides some support for the Allaire Report's suggestion that jurisdiction over labor policies, training, and postsecondary education should be given to Quebec. Since there is relatively little labor mobility between Quebec and the other provinces,[54] the magnitude of any externalities in these areas is probably smaller than the gains of having a locally determined and administered policy. Such a jurisdictional change may not be justified outside of Quebec, where the provinces may be tied more closely by migration. If you were born in the Atlantic provinces, there is about a 25 percent chance that you will live in another province, and there is one chance in eight that it will be Ontario. Atlantic Canadians traditionally abhor emigration, even though statistics show that their recent experience is similar to that of Western Canadians. There is a perception that migration in Western Canada is dominated by non-Westerners moving in and out with resource booms, and that few non-Westerners are forced to leave because of a lack of opportunities. While these perceptions are changing — especially in the light of Saskatchewan's experience — Atlantic Canada is perceived as being in steady decline, with many of its young, skilled workers being forced to seek employment outside their home province.

---

54 With continued constitutional uncertainty and language difficulties, the emigration of nonfrancophones from Quebec will likely disprove our generalization, at least in the short run.

Table 2:   *Out-Migration and*
**   *Attachment to Province of Birth, 1986***

	% of Those Born in the Province Continuing to Reside There	% of Population Moving Out of the Province
Newfoundland	74%	5.85
Prince Edward Island	68	6.30
Nova Scotia	75	5.50
New Brunswick	74	5.10
Quebec	92	1.79
Ontario	91	1.98
Manitoba	68	5.20
Saskatchewan	60	5.60
Alberta	79	8.47
British Columbia	88	4.80

Sources: Statistics Canada, *Ethnicity, Immigration and Citizenship*, Cat. no. 93-109; Canada, Department of Finance, "Economic Linkages among the Provinces," *Quarterly Economic Review* (1991), Table 11.A5.

While it is difficult to predict how constitutional reform will affect the ability of people to migrate, there appears to be a fairly straightforward connection between transfer changes and the incentives to migrate. It is only under the extreme scenario of total dissolution that we see the barriers to labor mobility increasing, and even then separate provinces may choose not to impede immigration. With increased education, and with the current calls for the removal of institutional barriers such as biased professional licensing, out-migration from the Atlantic region will become more feasible.

Migration is an important form of economic adjustment. Unimpeded migration should contribute to greater economic efficiency by facilitating the rational location of economic activities. Migration is also an element of social welfare, however, and is of particular concern to Atlantic Canadians who fear that they will bear the greatest cost of labor mobility. Transfer payments have permitted more people to stay in their home province than would otherwise be the case. It will be the treatment of transfers in the new Constitution that determines how strong the incentives will be to exploit the opportunity to move.

Table 3: **Out-Migration**
from the Atlantic Provinces, 1981–86
(percentage)

Province of Destination	Province of Origin			
	New-foundland	Prince Edward Island	Nova Scotia	New Brunswick
Newfoundland		3.8%	5.8%	2.4%
Prince Edward Island	1.7		4.1	3.7
Nova Scotia	18.8	25.6		21.0
New Brunswick	5.9	16.0	14.1	
Quebec	1.8	3.2	6.0	14.3
Ontario	47.7	25.4	40.9	32.7
Manitoba	2.8	2.5	3.1	3.5
Saskatchewan	1.2	1.5	1.6	1.8
Alberta	15.8	16.1	13.4	11.4
British Columbia	5.8	5.1	10.1	5.4

Note: Sums of out-migration to other provinces do not add to 100 percent due to rounding and the omission of the Yukon and Northwest Territories.

Sources: Statistics Canada, *Ethnicity, Immigration and Citizenship*, Cat. no. 93-109; Canada, Department of Finance, "Economic Linkages among the Provinces," *Quarterly Economic Review* (1991), Table 11.A5.

Simulation Results

This essay has concentrated on transfers as the key determinant of how constitutional reform will affect the economies of the Atlantic provinces. The following simulations were designed to represent varying degrees of transfer program changes in order to evaluate the magnitude of economic effects.

Numerous simulation exercises were performed in order to evaluate specific constitutional changes. We present only two of the more important simulation results here: the regionalization of the unemployment insurance program and fiscal autarky. The regionalization of UI requires contributions and benefits for the region to be equal; the results we present are for extreme cases of maintaining either current benefits by raising contributions, or of maintaining current contributions by lowering benefits. Obviously, an infinite number of compromises exists between these extremes. While UI reform is itself both important and probable, we may also use it as a proxy for other transfer changes of a similar magnitude.[55] The second major simulation imposes fiscal autarky by removing net transfers to the region from the rest of the country. This simulation could be used to represent either independence or a dramatically altered confederation in which net transfers between regions were eliminated.

The ideal way of estimating the impact of alternative policy scenarios would be through the use of a provincial/regional applied general equilibrium (AGE) model[56] combined with the insights that a model such as Statistics Canada's Social Policy Simulation Model could bring (it possesses the ability to describe the characteristics of the "winners" and "losers"). A regional example of such a model can be found in work carried out for the Macdonald Royal Commission.[57] This basic model has been updated for the use of the Economic Council of Canada, but was not available for use in this study. Instead, we use the recently developed Newfoundland and Labrador Econometric Model (NALEM).[58] The NALEM is essentially Keynesian, with neo-Classical long-run properties, and is based on the National Accounts. The NALEM emphasizes the supply side of the economy relative to most other models.

---

55 The correspondence between these UI reforms and other transfer reductions depends on the extent to which the income effects of transfer losses dominate the substitution effects. Changes to the form of a transfer program modifies the incentive structure in the economy, so that reducing net transfers through the UI program might have different effects than a reduction in equalization payments by a similar amount.

56 Any model is, however, constrained by data, economic theory, and econometric theory, and these constraints are constantly being changed.

57 See John Whalley and Irene Trela, *Regional Aspects of Confederation*, Collected Research Studies of the Royal Commission on the Economic Union and Development Prospects for Canada 68 (Toronto: University of Toronto Press, 1986).

58 The model was simulated by the staff at the Economic Research and Analysis Division, Executive Council, Government of Newfoundland and Labrador. All major assumptions about the control and shock solutions, and the simulation results themselves, are, however, the sole responsibility of the authors.

A major difference between the NALEM and most AGE models is the absence of nominal wage flexibility in the former. As a result, our estimates of the effects of decreasing transfer payments are larger than those predicted by an AGE model with flexible nominal wages, since most of the adjustment to a shock will be through quantity changes. In order to make a comparison, we required a "base case" scenario to develop indicators of future economic performance under "current" conditions. Two crucial assumptions underlie econometric models such as the one used here: (i) relationships observed in the past will continue into the future (for example, consumption expenditures will depend on disposable income and wealth); and (ii) events in the recent past are more important than those that occurred earlier. It has also been necessary for us to make arbitrary assumptions about major investment projects.[59]

While we recognize the dangers in using this model to characterize the region as a whole, we feel that a model of Newfoundland and Labrador serves as a reasonable proxy for the trends and orders of magnitude that would prevail in Atlantic Canada. Since the larger economies of New Brunswick and Nova Scotia are less dependent on transfers than Newfoundland, the effect on Atlantic Canada as a region will be lower than the numbers presented here. We suspect that most of the reported changes are approximately 30 percent higher than should be attributed to the Atlantic region as a whole.

Changes to the Unemployment Insurance Program

Our first simulation examines the impact of making the UI system self-financing at the provincial level. Since our estimates relate to Newfoundland, the province most dependent on UI transfers, we can consider this to be the worst-case scenario for the region.

---

59 Specifically, we have assumed that the Hibernia project would start producing in 1996, and that development of the Terra Nova fields and lower Churchill hydro-electric potential does not occur.

We consider two possible subcases: in the first, we permit UI benefits to be lowered to the level of contributions; in the second, we raise contributions to the projected level of benefits. The effects of the policy changes are shown in Table 4. The results are provided for the year 2000, which is the last year of our estimates.[60] In light of our previous discussion, the results are predictable. Reducing benefits leads to a marked reduction in real GDP and real per capita personal income. These estimates may even understate the true negative impact: cash flows from transfer payments are used to purchase intermediate goods and services for household production. The result is that the loss in a family's welfare level is much greater than the loss in transfer payments.[61] It should also be noted that, in the rural areas of the province, UI benefits can represent up to 40 percent of family income. The number of jobs is likely to fall more than predicted, since, with the reduction of benefits, job sharing would decrease and the number of "quits" would fall; in other words, employers and employees would abandon the "10-week" syndrome if at all possible. As was noted earlier, the decrease in real per capita income is minimized if there is out-migration. The importance of migration is highlighted by a comparison of cases A and B in Table 4. This comparison seems to support the position that national, rather than provincial, employment policies are desirable and that individuals should be given the opportunity to migrate.

When contributions to UI are raised to meet projected benefit levels, real per capita personal income actually increases. These unexpected results occur because the increasing premiums result in large negative corporate profits for all years. Even after employment is arbitrarily cut in seasonal industries, accounting for a large number of UI claimants, the negative profits persist.

These estimates of the economic effects do not take into account the distributional consequences of UI reform. In order to determine

---

60 By this year, most of the initial adjustment has taken place.

61 See S. May, "Appendix IV," in Newfoundland and Labrador, Royal Commission on Employment and Unemployment, *Building on Our Strengths* (St. John's: Queen's Printer, 1984).

Table 4: *Effects of a Provincial Unemployment Insurance Program on the Newfoundland Economy*
(percentage change from base)

	Reduced Benefits Scenarios		Increased Premiums Scenarios	
	Case A	Case B	Case A	Case B
Real GDP (constant 1981 dollars)	−10.1%	−12.8%	−7.9%	−11.9%
Real personal income per capita	−11.3	−3.2	4.1	9.5
Retail sales	−17.9	−23.6	−11.5	−20.4
Employment	−13.4	−16.2	−15.9	−20.5
Unemployment rate*	8.7	0.7	6.5	0.1
Population	−7.3	−19.8	−7.4	−20.5
GDP deflator	−0.2	−0.8	0.6	−0.3

Note: Case A and Case B simulations differ only in that a higher migration rate is assumed in the latter. The base unemployment rate is 10.4 percent for 2000, which is fairly optimistic given previous experience.

*Actual change, not percentage change from base.

the characteristics of the "losers", we examine the results from Statistic Canada's Social Policy Simulation Model (SPSM). While SPSM does not capture behavioral changes or the indirect effects of policy alterations, it does permit us to identify those income groups most affected by UI reforms. One study of the profile of current UI recipients for Newfoundland makes it clear that one could design a program that reduces benefits quite substantially in that province without significantly affecting those census families in the lower-income deciles.[62]

The same study states that UI recipients tend to be concentrated in a few occupations; for example, over 50 percent of the male claimants classify themselves as in construction, generally as laborers. Many of the claimants, both male and female, are fish-plant

---

62 See Michael Denny, Nancy Churchman, and David Weiss, "Reforming UI: Some Modest Experiments" (Paper prepared for the Newfoundland Department of Employment and Labour Relations, St. John's, 1990, Mimeographed). This study uses SPSM version 4 with 1986 data.

workers in the seasonal inshore plants. Men tend to use UI more than women, and the level of benefits they receive is higher. Older workers (over 55 years in age) tend to rely less on UI. Also, "the average benefit and the dependence on UI is much greater in the rural areas."[63] Almost 65 percent of the recipients were married with young children. In addition:

> UI benefits flow to the richer census families....The bottom 40 percent of census families receive only about 20 percent of the benefits, which is the same share as is received by the richest twenty percent of census families.[64]

The pattern is somewhat different for fishing benefits, with poorer families receiving relatively more than regular UI claimants, since "about one-half of them belong to the bottom 40 percent of the census family income distribution."[65]

There are several ways that benefits could be lowered to meet the present level of contributions within the province so that the program becomes self-financing (except for administrative costs). Benefit rates — that is, the proportion of insurable earnings that would be paid out as benefits — could be reduced. The current rate of 60 percent would be roughly reduced to 15 percent, assuming that employers' contributions are 1.4 times that of employee contributions. Presumably, the profile of recipients from this policy change would remain the same, and the various categories would be hit proportionally; using 1986 data, about 47 percent of the families in the province would be affected. If, on the other hand, the level of insurable earnings were reduced, there would be a larger impact on males living in rural areas at the upper-income levels, and only 43 percent of the families in the province would be affected. On the other hand, if employee contributions were to increase by about four times, almost 70 percent of the families would be affected.

---

63 Ibid., p. 7.

64 Ibid., p. 13.

65 Ibid., p. 17.

The message from these UI policy simulations is that the negative effects of policy changes arising out of constitutional reform could be directed to making the system more equitable and to protecting those most in need. These simulations also give the sense of how a partial reduction in net transfers would affect the Atlantic region.

Eliminating Net Transfers

In this simulation, we assume the dissolution of Canada and the absence of a federal government. As a result, federal savings drop to zero, and the present federal taxes collected in the provinces are taken over by the provincial governments. In order to accommodate the decrease in cash inflows, we make a number of arbitrary reductions in expenditures. All federal transfers to persons are reduced by 50 percent, as are current government expenditures on goods and services. UI benefits are reduced to the level of contributions. We stop all transfers to business. Gross fixed capital formation by governments, public institutions, and utilities are cut by one-half. We do not permit the size of the provincial deficit to increase. Given all these conditions, the residual becomes expenditures by the provincial government on current account. Although we formulate this scenario as a model of dissolution, the results would characterize the Atlantic region if Canada remained united but interregional transfers were eliminated.

This scenario has three subcases based on alternative assumptions about labor mobility. Case A assumes that the present pattern of out-migration continues. Case B assumes that the rate of out-migration responds more quickly to a reduction in job opportunities, and that the economic adjustment costs, psychic costs, or geographic preferences are all overcome. Case C is the "doomsday" scenario, in which migration slows as the other provinces restrict immigration from the Atlantic provinces. Table 5 presents the estimated impacts. Each observation represents the percentage change from the base case forecast for the province.

Table 5:   ***Effects of the Removal of Federal Transfers
on the Newfoundland Economy***
(percentage change from base)

	Case A		Case B		Case C	
	1993–97 average	2000	1993–97 average	2000	1993–97 average	2000
Real GDP (constant 1981 dollars)	–39.0%	–43.2%	–39.8%	–46.1%	–38.2%	–41.1%
Real personal income per capita	–34.7	–33.3	–6.8	–6.8	–38.0	–41.8
Retail sales	–41.5	–49.3	–48.4	–59.4	–39.8	–43.3
Employment	–44.6	–52.5	–44.7	–54.5	–44.1	–50.6
Unemployment rate*	30.9	31.8	2.9	4.3	34.3	40.8
Population	–9.2	–24.1	–43.6	–53.6	–1.3	–4.1
GDP deflator	–5.3	–4.8	–7.4	–7.3	–4.8	–3.3

Note: The base unemployment rate is 15.3 percent for the 1993–97 period and 10.4 percent for 2000. Therefore, in Case C, the unemployment rate in 2000 would be an astonishing 51.2 percent.

*Actual change, not percentage change from base.

Case A shows how dramatic the impact would be. Real per capita personal income would be 33.3 percent lower in the year 2000 because of the removal of transfers. This fall occurs even though there is substantial out-migration. By the year 2000, the population would be about 24 percent lower than the base case projection; that is, some 146,000 fewer people than in the base case. The reductions in population create a substantial negative shock to the residential construction sector. Faced with this disastrous scenario, the provincial government would be forced to be highly imaginative if it were to cushion the impact on the most disadvantaged groups. For example, UI benefits, family allowances, or old age pensions might be targeted to those most in need, or many employers and employees might work toward a reduction of wage rates in order to spread the impact.

A more detailed analysis of the impacts indicates that while exports are almost unaffected, imports fall dramatically. Overall consumer expenditures fall by over 45 percent in the year 2000. Those expenditures most affected include furniture and household appliances (down 84 percent), motor vehicles (down 56 percent), and restaurants (down 66 percent). The industrial impact, as expected, is uneven: commercial services (down 60 percent), trade (down 65 percent), and construction (down 50 percent) show some of the more dramatic decreases. Employment declines are equally dramatic, and while the decline is not that great in seasonal industries such as fishing, many employees may leave occupations in these sectors as UI benefits are cut.

These estimates require further fine tuning. For example, our methodology results in negative provincial government expenditures on goods and services. Obviously, in order for the government to operate in this world, provincial transfers to individuals would have to be cut further. However, we believe that the orders of magnitude of the changes are realistic and are supported by the casual evidence about the importance of federal activities in the Atlantic region.

In Case B, we force out-migration in order to prevent the unemployment rate from rising too dramatically; in this scenario, however, the province loses almost *54 percent* of its population. While the economy contracts more, due to the larger out-migration, real income on a per capita basis does not fall nearly as much as in Case A; the projected decline is 6.8 percent. In some of the intervening years, real personal per capita income actually rises. While labor is mobile, much of the physical capital is not, and one could therefore expect the losses to business to be much greater than those predicted by this model. Not all persons are equally mobile, however, and those who are older or have less formal education are likely to remain where they are. There is ample evidence showing that in single-industry towns when the company closes the period of adjustment is often long. Families are often thrown into a poverty trap to which they may be consigned for generations.

Case C is the doomsday scenario in which out-migration is slowed. The situation is somewhat similar to that existing in Newfoundland during the 1930s, when immigration into Canada and the

United States was restricted and many Newfoundlanders were forced to return home when temporary work permits were not renewed. Case C shows real per capita income declining by almost 42 percent. There are declines in levels of employment, retail sales, and real output, and these declines are larger than under the "forced migration" scenario of Case B.

The conclusion seems to be that the degree to which individuals are affected in an economic sense depends on the extent to which and the ease with which either they or their fellow citizens can move elsewhere. *The assumptions about migration are crucial if one wants to estimate the decline in individual well-being.* Interestingly, it would seem to be the owners of equity and fixed capital who would bear the largest burden if there were to be massive out-migration. Presumably, under large-scale out-migration many businesses would be forced to close.

Conclusions

The Allaire Report, the majority of the Canadian business community, and perhaps even a majority of Canadians are calling for increased regional ties through free interprovincial trade, and decreased regional ties based on dependency-inducing transfer payments from the rich provinces to the poor. These calls appear to be based on the same *laissez-faire* principles that have led to greater North American and international economic integration, and may prove to be equally compelling. The movement toward an "economically" rational Constitution, however, may not be along a smooth and continuous curve of the type economists prefer: there may be a serious political discontinuity in our path. We must be careful not to break the social contract that has held us together until now; too much economically rational integration may lead to political disintegration. Unfortunately — as the current constitutional debate has highlighted — the Canadian social contract may mean fundamentally different things to different people.

Insofar as Atlantic Canadians can be portrayed as having similar constitutional views, we have argued that transfer payments make up a critical component of the social contract and may, perhaps, have been the single most important issue in persuading the Maritimes initially — and Newfoundland eventually — to enter into Confederation.[66] Their perceptions were not without foundation: Term 29 of the Terms of Union between Newfoundland and Canada is echoed in Section 36(2) of the *Constitution Act*.

Constitutions change, and one of Canada's traditional strengths has been a constitution sufficiently flexible to permit compromise. However, there is no guarantee that a constitution will be perpetually consistent with the aspirations of its citizens. Canada has reached the point where its provinces must decide which sacrifices can be tolerated to accommodate Confederation, and which are too great to justify continued political union.

How flexible can Atlantic Canada afford to be on the question of transfers? This paper has painted a fairly bleak picture of an Atlantic Canada devoid of financial assistance from the other provinces. Its economic structure is resource based and largely inflexible; adjusting vigorously to adverse economic shocks has not been a traditional strength of the Atlantic Canadian economy. Mitigating this pessimistic assessment is the fact that Atlantic Canadians have proved themselves to be capable of enduring extreme economic hardship when necessary and have demonstrated a propensity for taking advantage of any opportunities that do arise.[67]

Atlantic Canada is likely to accept — at least in theory — the need to make transfer programs more consistent with the principles of economic efficiency. Its argument will be about the level of net transfers to the region. While the abuse of transfer programs and the

---

66 The fact that 80 years passed before Maritimers were joined in Confederation by Newfoundlanders does result in differences between their expectations. When the Maritime provinces entered Confederation, public services were less extensive and transfer payments were less ubiquitous and geared toward infrastructure such as investment in improved transportation. In 1949, social services were more developed, and Newfoundlanders had a more precise understanding of what services and transfers they could expect.

67 For an example, consider how the UI program has been integrated into the local economies.

dependency that has been generated are detested by the majority of both recipients and donors, the abuses have also been tolerated. A precipitous reduction in transfers will lead to an extremely painful period of transition. Atlantic Canadians should therefore be concerned about both the speed and size of any adjustment. Income security programs should be redesigned so as to conform to basic principles of equity, self-reliance, community development, and efficiency. Society may not owe the disadvantaged a living in the manner in which we have traditionally provided one. But if we have participated in a system that has led some people to believe that we do, then changing the rules of the game without making provisions for the adjustment of expectations would seem to violate the principles of justice with which Canadians traditionally have identified themselves. Indeed, the timing of program changes may be the dimension of the debate needed to assure agreement on fundamental constitutional questions.[68]

Our analysis shows that any change in Canadian Confederation tending to diminish federal government dollar inflows will, *ceteris paribus*, have a direct and immediate negative impact on the standard of living in the region. The reduction in dependency would also force these economies to react more to market forces and would make Atlantic Canadians more susceptible to income fluctuations. Reduced real personal incomes will also lead to greater out-migration. Economists Rick Harris and Doug Purvis remind us that "the key point is that these transfer payments serve as a substitute for labor mobility as a way of adjusting to economic shocks."[69]

---

68 It is possible that the presence of extraordinary revenues from oil and gas developments off the east coast could be of considerable importance in assisting the region in its adjustment to a new transfer regime. The revenues would induce declines in transfers anyway, which might relieve the pressure for reforming transfer programs. Receipts are unlikely to begin prior to any constitutional settlement, however, because of the deadlines evolving in Quebec. We would like to see the transfer programs reformed and the revenues from oil and gas used to facilitate the transition.

69 Richard G. Harris and Douglas D. Purvis, "Some Economic Aspects of Political Restructuring" (Paper presented at the conference, "The Economic Dimensions of Constitutional Change," sponsored by the John Deutsch Institute for the Study of Economic Policy, Kingston, Ont., June 4–6, 1991, Mimeographed).

Although enhanced prospects for mobility increase the opportunities for individual Atlantic Canadians, and should only lead to an increase in the welfare of the migrants, the provincial governments of the region will regard emigration as a threat to their economy, culture, and constitutional status. Reducing the incentive to migrate was a goal the Atlantic provinces had when they entered Confederation; it was the fear of increased marginalization through depopulation that permeated Atlantic Canada's agenda for the Canadian social contract. These concerns are still present; any politician from the Atlantic provinces publicly accepting massive out-migration from that region would be committing political suicide. Canadians must decide where along the transfer-migration continuum they are willing to move in order to accommodate each other.

We do not know the levels of transfers and migration each region is willing to tolerate. The only common ground that does stand out is that the form of transfer programs must be changed to minimize dependency-inducing incentives; the UI system is the most obvious candidate for reform. Transfers of income also require efficiency-reducing taxes, so there may be compelling fiscal and efficiency arguments for reducing the net levels of transfers to the region. Atlantic Canadians must recognize the need for transfer program changes and transfer reductions. The danger of a constitutional debacle that could lead to the precipitous elimination of all transfers is a powerful incentive to be flexible on other aspects of the constitution. The rest of Canada, however, should recognize that the cost of making transfers to the Atlantic region is fairly small, and that the cost of ensuring a smooth transition to lower transfer levels is even smaller. While we cannot say how much transfers should or will be reduced, we do think that the rest of Canada should finance a gradual adjustment to reduce hardship in the region and to accommodate changes in migration patterns.[70]

---

70 Political changes in Eastern Europe and restructuring programs in less-developed countries have highlighted the debate between gradual adjustment and using "shock" treatment. We are not arguing in favor of the former. The incentive structures of current transfer programs should be adjusted quickly, but the transfer levels should be reduced more gradually.

While economic rationality has appeared to prevail in recent years, the Canadian electorate has not yet embraced the value system of a purely market-driven economy. As much as we may be willing to shake it cordially, we still fear the slap of Adam Smith's invisible hand. International reality will circumscribe our ability to avoid the rigors of a pure market, but we are still willing to make sacrifices in order to protect our culture and our communities. Canadians understand the noneconomic factors affecting their well-being; these factors encouraged them to set up an independent country as an alternative to simply joining friends and relatives in the United States. Quebec Premier Robert Bourassa is also sympathetic to the concept of protecting culture, language, and a unique value system. Whether we like it or not, economic trade and factor mobility has a tendency to reduce the cultural differences we celebrate.[71] It is clear that the current economic system of transfers and barriers to trade and factor mobility have permitted the provinces in the Atlantic region to have larger populations and political bargaining strength than would be the case had economic efficiency prevailed earlier.

The constitutional debate over transfers will appear most visibly as a regional conflict. However, we should not be deceived into thinking that transfer programs are an Atlantic Canadian concern alone. Transfers, migration, and culture are all inextricably linked, and the constitutional reform process must address the tradeoffs between these conflicting goals even in the absence of regional disagreements. The way Canada accommodates the aspirations of the Atlantic provinces will largely define how Canadians write the social contract among income classes as well.

---

71 To discuss the matter further, we could meet at McDonald's in Ste-Foy.

Appendix Tables:

Atlantic Canada's Exports, Imports, and Trade Balance, 1984

Table A-1: *Atlantic Canada's Exports, by Destination, 1984*
($ millions)

Sector	Destination of Exports			
	Quebec	Ontario and Western Canada	Canada (total)	Rest of World
Agriculture	181.0	332.3	513.3	191.6
Mining	93.3	138.8	232.1	866.5
Forestry	110.2	204.8	315.0	1,569.9
Fish, meat	52.4	75.2	127.6	998.1
Total primary	*436.9*	*751.1*	*1,188.0*	*3,626.1*
Beverages	22.2	12.4	34.6	46.5
Textiles	183.9	119.2	303.1	274.3
Metal manufacturing	225.3	256.1	481.4	433.7
Other manufacturing	72.5	101.0	173.5	143.8
Total secondary	*503.9*	*488.7*	*992.6*	*898.3*
Fuel	350.5	46.9	397.4	392.9
Utilities	108.0	0.0	108.0	378.3
Total fuel and utilities	*458.5*	*46.9*	*505.4*	*771.2*
Transportation, communications	912.8	1,074.8	1,987.6	211.5
Financial services	265.7	215.7	481.4	6.2
Other services	229.8	255.0	484.8	303.3
Total services	*1,408.3*	*1,545.5*	*2,953.8*	*521.0*
Other	0.0	0.0	0.0	53.7
Total	*2,807.6*	*2,832.2*	*5,639.8*	*5,870.3*

Table A-2: *Atlantic Canada's Imports,*
               by Source, 1984
               ($ millions)

Sector	Source of Imports			
	Quebec	Ontario and Western Canada	Canada (total)	Rest of World
Agriculture	208.8	547.7	756.5	191.9
Mining	197.1	60.9	258.0	33.1
Forestry	298.6	329.9	628.5	79.4
Fish, meat	178.8	232.3	411.1	175.7
Total primary	*883.3*	*1,170.8*	*2,054.1*	*480.1*
Beverages	11.8	43.3	55.1	38.6
Textiles	549.8	527.7	1,077.5	117.6
Metal manufacturing	437.0	1,058.2	1,495.2	2,058.8
Other manufacturing	752.2	1,397.5	2,149.7	742.0
Total secondary	*1,750.8*	*3,026.7*	*4,777.5*	*2,957.0*
Fuel	588.2	71.0	659.2	2,285.3
Utilities	124.4	0.0	124.4	0.1
Total fuel and utilities	*712.6*	*71.0*	*783.6*	*2,285.4*
Transportation, communications	513.4	853.3	1,366.7	71.7
Financial services	442.6	98.4	542.0	1.8
Other services	814.7	1,785.1	2,599.8	344.7
Total services	*1,771.7*	*2,736.8*	*4,508.5*	*418.2*
Other	0.0	0.0	0.0	323.1
Total	*5,118.4*	*7,005.3*	*12,123.7*	*6,6463.8*

Table A-3: *Atlantic Canada's Trade Balance, by Partner, 1984*
($ millions)

Sector	Trade Balance				
	Quebec	Ontario and Western Canada	Canada (total)	Rest of World	Total
Agriculture	(27.8)	(215.4)	(243.2)	2.2	(241.0)
Mining	77.9	(103.8)	(25.9)	833.5	807.6
Forestry	(188.4)	(125.1)	(313.5)	1,491.4	1,177.9
Fish, meat	(126.4)	(157.1)	(283.5)	824.1	540.6
Total primary	*(446.4)*	*(419.7)*	*(866.1)*	*3,151.2*	*2,285.1*
Beverages	10.4	(30.9)	(20.5)	8.0	(12.5)
Textiles	(365.9)	(408.5)	(774.4)	158.1	(616.3)
Metal manufacturing	(211.7)	(802.1)	(1,013.8)	(1,594.0)	(2,607.8)
Other manufacturing	(679.7)	(1,296.5)	(1,976.2)	(591.5)	(2,567.7)
Total secondary	*(1,246.9)*	*(2,538.0)*	*(3,784.9)*	*(2,019.4)*	*(5,804.3)*
Fuel	(237.7)	(24.1)	(261.8)	(1,892.2)	(2,154.0)
Utilities	916.4)	0.0	(16.4)	378.2	361.8
Total fuel and utilities	*(254.1)*	*(24.1)*	*(278.2)*	*(1,514.0)*	*(1,792.2)*
Transportation, communications	399.4	221.5	620.9	140.4	761.3
Financial services	(177.9)	117.3	(60.6)	4.4	(56.2)
Other services	(584.9)	(1,530.1)	(2,115.0)	(41.3)	(2,156.3)
Total services	*(363.4)*	*(1,191.3)*	*(1,554.7)*	*103.5*	*(1,451.2)*
Other	0.0	0.0	0.0	(268.4)	(268.4)
Total	*(2,310.8)*	*(4,173.1)*	*(6,483.9)*	*(547.1)*	*(7,031.0)*

Notes on the Appendix Tables

The data in the three appendix tables are based on Statistics Canada's Input-Output Tables for 1984, using the following Statistics Canada sectoral categories:

1. Grains
2. Other agricultural products
3. Forestry products
4. Fishing and trapping products
5. Metallic ores and concentrates
6. Minerals, fuels
7. Nonmetallic minerals
8. Services incidental to mining
9. Meat, fish and dairy products
10. Fruit, vegetables, feed, miscellaneous food products
11. Beverages
12. Tobacco and tobacco products
13. Rubber, leather, plastic fabricated products
14. Textile products
15. Knitted products and clothing
16. Lumber, sawmill and other wood products
17. Furniture and fixtures
18. Paper and paper products
19. Printing and publishing
20. Primary metal products
21. Metal fabricated products
22. Machinery and equipment
23. autos, trucks and other transportation equipment
24. Electronic and communications products
25. Nonmetallic mineral products

26. Petroleum and coal products
27. Chemicals and chemical products
28. Miscellaneous manufactured products
29. Residential construction
30. Nonresidential construction
31. Repair construction
32. Transportation and storage
33. Communications services
34. Other utilities
35. Wholesale margins
36. Retail margins
37. Imputed rent from owner-occupied dwellings
38. Other finance, insurance and real estate
39. Business services
40. Personal and other miscellaneous services
41. Transportation margins
42. Operating, office, lab and food
43. Travel, advertising, promotion
44. Noncompeting imports
45. Unallocated imports and exports
46. Net indirect taxes
47. Labor income
48. Net income from unincorporated businesses
49. Other operating surplus

The sectors denoted in the tables are composed of the following lines:

Agriculture consists of categories 1, 2, and 10.
Mining consists of categories 5, 7, and 8.
Forestry consists of categories 3, 16, 17, and 18.
Fishing consists of categories 4 and 9.
Beverages is category 11.
Textiles consists of categories 13, 14, and 15.
Metal manufacturing consists of categories 20, 21, 22, and 23.
Other manufacturing consists of categories 12, 19, 24, 25, 27, and 28.
Fuel consists of categories 6 and 26.
Utilities is category 34.
Transportation and communications consists of categories 32, 33, and 41.
Financial services is category 38.
Other services consists of categories 25, 36, 39, 40, 42, and 43.
Other consists of categories 44 and 45.

It should be noted that some of these categories have been selected to concentrate on particularly interesting sectors for the Atlantic Canada economy, and probably would not be appropriate for other provincial economies.

A Comment

E.J. Chambers and M.B. Percy

Doug May and Dane Rowlands provide a comprehensive overview of the economic structure of Atlantic Canada and the pervasive growing role of the federal government in maintaining it. The authors are thorough in their review of the contribution of federal transfer programs to the region and in assessing the consequences for economic efficiency that follow. The Atlantic region is modeled as a small open economy, a structure that provides the framework for evaluating the region's adjustment to movements in its terms of trade or its trade deficit with and without federal transfers.

It is a sobering experience to read the paper. The data clearly demonstrate the precarious nature of the Atlantic economy and its vulnerability to shifts in the structure of fiscal federalism. Yet one is struck also by the nature of the Atlantic vision — how best to ensure that federal policies offset the market adjustments that would normally correct a trade deficit as large and as sustained as the Atlanatic region's. What is depressing is that May and Rowlands assess the mechanisms of adjustment — changes in trade patterns, transfers, and migration — solely in terms of their costs to the level of economic activity in the region. They ignore the benefits of permitting these adjustments to occur in terms of potential income gains to all Canadians. In this Atlantic view, the rest of Canada is nothing more than a foreign-aid donor without the right to seek structural adjustments by the recipient.

While federal programs do permit a larger Atlantic economy to exist than would otherwise be the case, they do so at the cost of lost output in the rest of Canada because of the diversion of capital and labor to the Atlantic region. There are also the efficiency costs associated with raising the additional tax revenues necessary to fund federal transfers.

The perverse nature of the Atlantic vision is evident in the discussion of productivity improvements. May and Rowlands see improved labor productivity as increasing unemployment with no corresponding increase in output elsehere in the region. Hence, they do not view improved productivity as the mechanism for improving real incomes. Yet, if the next-best alternative for displaced workers in the Atlantic region is employment elsewhere in Canada, then real incomes in Canada as a whole would rise and the economic well-being of the remaining residents of the Atlantic region could also increase.

There are gains to Canada's regions from membership in the Canadian economic union, especially from the (potential) benefits of economic stabilization and enhanced international market power. Yet these gains can be dissipated if the union's policies focus more on offsetting the mechanisms of regional adjustment as they come into play in response to persistent and large regional trade deficits. At some point, the costs of maintaining the economic union may exceed the benefits of economic integration in aggregate or from the perspective of a particular region. The debate on constitutional reform following the collapse of the Meech Lake Accord provides a welcome opportunity to assess the current structure of the economic union.

Natural Resources and the Western Canadian Economy: Implications for Constitutional Change

E.J. Chambers and M.B. Percy

The failure to ratify the Meech Lake Accord in the summer of 1990 has led to a period of intense evaluation by individual Canadians, various provincial constitutional task forces, and an array of federal government task forces and commissions of what is expected of the Canadian Confederation. In part, the focus of these discussions — and their timing — has been determined by Quebec's clearly articulated vision of a far more decentralized Confederation, one which meets its perceived economic and political needs. Though Quebec has been successful in highlighting the nature of the constitutional change it desires, there has been little discussion of what other regions of the country might want, given their own special characteristics. Rather, with some exceptions,[1] the various constitutional scenarios have often been in the context of "the Rest of Canada" (ROC) and Quebec. Clearly, ROC is not a homogeneous economic and political entity, and it is misleading to treat it as such.

This paper focuses on the economic structure of Western Canada and addresses distinctive features of the region that should be considered in the discussion of constitutional change. The paper is

---

1 See, for example, Paul Boothe, "The Economics of Association: A Regional Approach to Constitutional Design," Research Paper 91-11 (Edmonton, University of Alberta, Department of Economics, 1991); and Thomas J. Courchene, "The Community of the Canadas" (Kingston, Ont., Queen's University, Institute of Intergovernmental Relations, 1991).

unabashedly empirical in nature, and draws heavily on work either completed or in progress at the Western Centre for Economic Research at the University of Alberta.[2] Its purpose is to demonstrate the continuing importance of natural resources to Western Canada and to offer an overview of some of the economic consequences that follow. This provides the framework for policymakers in Western Canada to use when assessing revisions to the current structure of the economic union.

The discussion proceeds as follows. The next section briefly describes the nature of the economic gains that derive from Confederation and highlights the most important from the perspective of Western Canada. We then examine key features of the Western Canadian economy, looking first at industrial structure and employment, then turning to the region's structure of international trade. This is followed by an assessment of the consequences of continuing economic specialization in natural resources for an array of provincial variables. The evidence is that specialization in natural resources increases the economic variability of the provincial economies and that it does so through a variety of channels — especially commodity prices, exchange rates, and rates of capital formation. In the final section, we ask whether the present Canadian economic union accommodates the distinctive features of the Western Canadian economy and if the region could better address these problems on its own.

The Gains from Economic Integration

The literature on the economic aspects of Confederation draws heavily from international trade theory to outline the potential gains

---

2 A preliminary version of this paper was presented at "Western Economists Meeting on the Constitution," University of Alberta, May 24–25, 1991. This paper draws heavily on work presented in E.J. Chambers and Michael Percy, *Western Canada in the International Economy*, Western Studies in Economic Policy 2 (Edmonton: Western Centre for Economic Research, forthcoming); and idem, "Structural Characteristics of the Alberta Economy: Implications for Constitutional Scenarios" (Paper prepared for the conference, "Alberta and the Economics of Constitutional Change," University of Alberta, Edmonton, September 28, 1991).

in real income — the "economic surplus" — that derive from the arrangement and how this potential income gain can be dissipated through "balkanization". The basic approach is to describe the various stages of economic integration possible among countries and to suggest the sources of real income gains as one moves to successively greater integration.[3] A free trade area — in which the participating countries remove all barriers to trade in goods and services among themselves but each maintains its separate, pre-agreement trade barriers with nonparticipating regions — is the lowest degree of economic integration. The next stage of integration, a customs union, is merely a free trade area in which the participants agree to common trade barriers with the rest of the world. The next highest stage of integration, a common market, includes all the features of a customs union with the further provision that all participants agree to the unhindered flow of capital and labor among member countries.

An economic union such as the Canadian federation moves beyond the integration of markets into the realm of the integration of policy instruments by participating members (the provinces). An economic union has all of the characteristics of a common market, includes a monetary union, and provides for harmonization or integration of policy instruments at a level compatible with the political structure chosen by participating members to allocate government functions. In Canada's case, there is a relatively high degree of decentralization of economic policy instruments to the participating provinces.

What, then, are the sources of economic gain from greater integration? It has been suggested that there are four basic gains from an economic union such as Confederation.[4]

The first set of gains derives from the incentives for greater specialization of labor and the exploitation of scale economies be-

---

3 See Kenneth Norrie, Richard Simeon, and Mark Krasnick, *Federalism and the Economic Union*, collected Research Studies of the Royal Commission on the Economic Union and Development Prospects for Canada 56 (Toronto: University of Toronto Press, 1986).

4 Judith Maxwell and Caroline Pestieau, *Economic Realities of Contemporary Confederation*, Accent Quebec 14 (Montreal: C.D. Howe Research Institute, 1980).

cause of the elimination of barriers to interregional trade and the free flow of capital and labor. The larger market of the economic union permits a more efficient allocation of labor and other factors among sectors and regions. The result is greater specialization, improved productivity, and higher real incomes.

The second source of gains is the ability to pool risks at the national level to ameliorate the consequences of regional instability. This pooling includes creating interregional insurance and transfer programs, changing labor and capital flows among regions in response to varying economic opportunities, and designing macroeconomic stabilization policies aimed at particular regions. National risk pooling is a highly valuable feature of an economic union. It permits regions to specialize in those areas of production in which they are most efficient, while providing mechanisms of insurance against some of the costs of such specialization. In the short run, the tax base of the economic union — which is broader than that of the smaller region — permits transfers, by way of the federal government, from regions whose economies are expanding to those whose economies are in recession. In the longer run, labor mobility is the ultimate insurance for residents of regions whose economic base is in decline.

The third source of economic gains from Confederation is the sharing of overhead expenditures on defense, the provision of justice, large-scale transportation projects, and similar areas of mutual benefit to the partners in the economic union.

The final source of gains is the greater market power that an economic union can exert in international trade relations. Bigger and more diversified economies are often successful in trade negotiations because of both their sheer size and their ability to engage in more economic tradeoffs than is possible for smaller, less-diversified regions. An economic union can use this market power to increase export prices or reduce import prices, thus improving its terms of trade and increasing the real income of its residents.

Confederation, then, does seem to offer the potential of increasing the real incomes of provinces and their residents because of the benefits derived from regional integration. Would benefits of similar or greater magnitude be available, however, to the participating regions through alternate trading arrangements? It is important to realize that the magnitude of the potential surplus derived from Confederation is not a constant. Its size varies as a result of changes in Canada that influence the structure of the economy and the mechanisms of interregional adjustment and external factors — such as foreign tariffs, transportation costs — that offset the possibility of trade with other countries.

From this perspective, it is highly likely that two sources of the economic surplus — the gains from trade and the sharing of overheads — are probably not important to Western Canada. The Canada-U.S. Free Trade Agreement (FTA) and the possibility of continued trade liberalization through multinational vehicles such as the General Agreement on Tariffs and Trade mean that Western Canada can capture many of the gains from specialization and scale through international trade rather than through trade with other regions of Canada. In fact, to the extent that interregional trade in Canada is a consequence of trade diversion arising from Canadian barriers to international trade, it may be costly relative to trade with external partners. The sharing of overheads may also no longer be an important source of economic gain to Western Canada. The logic of greater trade liberalization, particularly as exemplified by the FTA, means that north-south linkages may become more important than the traditional east-west ones. The existing economic union is probably not well structured to deal with this new orientation.

The two remaining sources of economic surplus from Confederation — the insurance gains and greater market power — are likely to be very important to the economic well-being of Western Canada. The evidence to follow in the next two sections suggests a highly volatile economy in which economic stabilization and insurance aspects of an economic union are crucial, an economy whose specialization in and geographic concentration of exports makes it particularly susceptible to trade harassment.

Distributional considerations are also crucial. From the perspective of any one region, it is not the size of the economic surplus

accruing in aggregate to the economic union that is important, but
the share of the economic surplus that the region receives and the
efficacy of the institutional structure that distributes the benefits of
economic integration.

Resources in the
Western Canadian Economy

The following two sections are empirical in nature and cover much
factual material. Thus, we simply highlight what we believe are the
main points to emerge from the evidence.

The Distribution of Employment

As of 1988, employment in Western Canada contrasted with the
national data in a number of ways, the most important of which are
the following:

- The share of agriculture was 6.9 percent, or approximately twice
  the national average.
- Those people who had jobs in nonagricultural primary industries amounted to 4.1 percent of total employment, compared
  with a national average of 2.5 percent.
- Only 10.1 percent of jobs were in manufacturing, compared
  with 17.2 percent nationally.

The distribution of employment in the construction and service
industries, however, resembled the national average.

The comparison of employment across the four Western provinces also indicates striking differences. In the three Prairie provinces, agriculture's relative importance is more than twice as great
in Saskatchewan as in Alberta and Manitoba. In all Western provinces, the proportion of employment in nonagricultural primary
industry exceeds the national average — more in Alberta than in the
other three provinces because of the size of its energy sector. While
all four provinces have smaller shares of employment in manufac-

Table 1: *Major Western Canadian Merchandise Exports, 1986–89 Average*
(as a percentage of total exports)

Commodity	% Share of Total Exports
Crude petroleum	11.73%
Sawn softwood lumber	11.08
Wood pulp	9.29
Wheat	8.04
Natural gas	7.59
Coal	5.11
Newsprint	2.75
Potash	2.48
Copper ores and concentrates	1.98
Sulphur	1.82
Fish	1.51
Canola	1.40
Aluminum	1.39
Paperboard	1.38
Total	*67.55*

Source: Statistics Canada, *Exports by Country*, Cat. no. 65-003, various issues.

turing than the national average, manufacturing is relatively more important in British Columbia and Manitoba.

Merchandise Trade Links with the Rest of the World

Table 1 provides an overview of Western Canada's major exports during the 1986–89 period. What is striking is that six primary commodities account for more than one-half of total export values. When 23 other export groups are added to the top six in the table, some 85 percent of the West's total international exports are covered. Most of these additional export categories consist of unprocessed and processed primary commodities.

Table 2 profiles each of the Western provinces' five leading exports to the international economy in 1986 and 1987. The striking feature here is the dominant position of unprocessed and processed

Table 2:   *Western Canada's Leading*
                Commodity Exports by Province, 1986 and 1987
                (as a percentage of total exports)

Commodity	1986	1987
Manitoba		
Wheat	23.55%	14.20%
Flaxseed (1986); nickel and alloys (1987)	4.04	6.12
Electricity (1986); aircraft parts (1987)	4.51	4.05
Lumber products (1986); motor vehicle parts (1987)	3.55	3.73
Canola	3.29	3.17
Total	39.74	31.27
Saskatchewan		
Wheat	28.31	26.50
Crude petroleum	16.96	20.04
Potash	13.08	13.08
Canola	3.76	3.56
Wood pulp	2.81	3.38
Total	64.92	66.56
Alberta		
Crude petroleum	27.16	30.26
Natural gas	21.51	19.26
Sulphur	5.33	4.78
Wheat	4.62	4.52
Coal	3.19	3.07
Total	61.81	61.89
British Columbia		
Sawn and planed lumber	23.38	25.72
Wood pulp	13.99	17.08
Coal	11.37	7.83
Newsprint	6.52	5.90
Copper ores and concentrates	3.41	3.63
Total	58.67	60.16

Source: Statistics Canada, *Exports by Country*, Cat. no. 65-003, various issues.

primary commodities. Only in Manitoba did secondary manufactured products enter the list, and this was only for one year.

Given the heavy concentration of the region's major exports in
just six categories and the evidence of similar concentration at the
provincial level (although varying by product across provinces), it
is not surprising that market slumps for just a few primary products

Table 3: *Foreign Markets for*
Western Canadian Exports, 1986–88 Average
(percentage shares, by destination)

| Market | Exporter | | | | | |
	British Columbia	Alberta	Sask-atchewan	Manitoba	Western Canada	All Canada
United States	44.97%	71.55%	39.74%	57.07%	54.06%	75.30%
Japan	26.30	6.54	10.63	7.63	15.93	5.76
Other Pacific Rim	7.19	4.68	4.64	2.36	5.59	2.72
Western Europe	13.40	2.59	6.23	10.45	8.50	8.33
Latin America	1.36	1.65	3.79	2.00	1.86	0.82
Central America	0.66	1.16	3.34	2.73	1.36	1.26
USSR & Eastern Europe	0.20	2.87	10.75	6.16	3.13	1.07
China	1.61	2.94	11.41	5.87	3.82	1.36
Middle East	0.25	1.34	4.25	2.84	1.40	0.43
Africa	0.35	2.31	2.60	0.96	1.38	0.78
Other Asia	0.66	0.74	1.66	1.02	0.86	0.72
Australia, New Zealand, Oceania	2.97	1.60	1.01	0.88	2.09	1.12

Note: Totals may not add to 100.00 because of rounding.

Source: Statistics Canada, *Exports by Country*, Cat. no. 65-003, various issues.

cast a pall over the region while favorable market conditions in the same products generate a "boom" atmosphere.

The Spatial Distribution of Markets

Table 3 provides a profile of the geographic distribution of international export markets for the Western provinces, for the region as a whole, and for Canada. Two features stand out. First, the U.S. market is relatively less important and the Japanese market relatively more important for Western Canada than for the country as a whole; even in Alberta, where the share of exports going to the United States is similar

Table 4: *Western Canada's Share of World Production and Exports of Selected Commodities*
(percentage share, volume basis)

Commodity	% Share of World Production	% Share of World Exports
Copper ores and concentrates	5%	9%
Natural gas	5	5
Crude oil	2	8
Sawn and planed lumber	10	38
Paper and paperboard	1	4
Wood pulp	3	14
Sulphur (all forms)	12	45
Zinc ores and concentrates	11	11
Potash	25	40
Wheat	5	20
Canola	17	43
Barley	8	24

Note: Western Canada's exports of natural gas and crude oil to the United States represent 1 percent of the U.S. market for each commodity.

Sources: Canada, Department of Energy, Mines and Resources, *Statistical Summary of the Mineral Industry in Canada 1987*; Canada, Statistics Canada, *Exports by Country*, Cat. no. 65-003, various issues; idem, *Exports by Province*, Cat. no. 36-204, various issues; idem, *Pulp and Paper Industries 1984*, Cat. no. 36-204; idem, *Sawmills and Planing Mills and Shingle Mills 1984*, Cat. no. 35-204; Organisation for Economic Co-operation and Development, *Annual Oil and Gas Statistics* various issues; idem, *Imports by Commodity*, various issues; United Nations Food and Agriculture Organization, *Yearbook of Agricultural Production 1988*; idem, *Yearbook of Forest Products 1984*; idem, *Yearbook of Trade and Commerce in Agricultural Products 1988*; United Nations, UNCTAD, *Commodity Yearbook 1987*; United States, Department of the Interior, Bureau of Mines, *Minerals Yearbook 1987*.

to the Canadian average, the commodity composition of the exports differs dramatically. Second, the relative importance of the different export markets varies substantially among the four provinces.

Western Canada's Production and Export Shares in the World Context

Table 4 shows that Western Canada does appear to have some degree of market power in a range of selected export markets, because it accounts for a significant share of world exports. Potash, sulphur,

Table 5: *Commodity Exports of the Western Provinces as a Share of Provincial GDP, 1986–87 Average*

	Foreign Exports as a % of Provincial GDP	Total Exports as a % of Provincial GDP
British Columbia	24.5%	33.1%
Alberta	19.5	39.0
Saskatchewan	27.4	40.4
Manitoba	13.4	30.4

Sources: Statistics Canada, *Provincial Economic Accounts*, Cat. no. 13-213, various issues; idem, *Exports by Country*, Cat. no. 65-003, various issues.

canola (rapeseed), and sawn and planed lumber fall into this category. In the case of energy, especially natural gas, Western Canada has market power in particular U.S. regional markets.

The West's concentration in a narrow range of primary products (Table 1) — differentiated from other competitors more by price than by quality — combined with its share in international markets (Table 4) has an important implication for the nature of competition in these markets. Western exporters must compete not only with domestic producers in those markets into which Canadian producers ship, but also with producers in "third countries".

The Contribution of Exports to Provincial GDP

Table 5 provides a measure of the contribution of foreign exports and total exports to provincial GDP. The relative importance of interprovincial exports is the difference between columns 2 and 1. Not only does the importance of total exports vary significantly among the provinces, so does the relative importance of interprovincial and international markets for them.

Figure 1 focuses on the relative contribution of interprovincial exports to provincial GDP. Since it is likely that at least some of these manufactured exports destined for markets in the rest of Canada could be sold in foreign markets, one can treat these data as provid-

Figure 1: *Shares of Interprovincial Manufacturing*
Exports in Provincial GDP, Western Canada, 1967–84

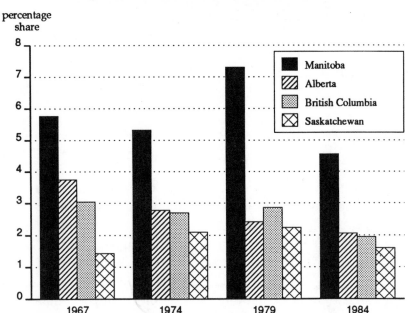

Source: Statistics Canada, *Canadian Economic Observer*, Cat. no. 11-010, various issues; and
idem, *Manufacturing Industries of Canada, National and Provincial Areas*, Cat. no. 31-203,
various issues.

ing an upper-bound estimate of the contribution of interprovincial
exports to provincial income. It is upper bound in that some of this
trade is trade diversion within the economic union. These are small
shares indeed.

Economic Consequences of the
West's Resource Specialization

Variability in Prices

Table 6 illustrates the degree to which prices in the markets for raw
and semiprocessed materials are more volatile than those in markets
for finished goods. For comparative purposes, the table provides

Table 6: *Volatility of the Prices of Main Export Groups and Finished Goods*
(deviation of quarterly price changes, 1972:1Q–1988:2Q)

Sector Price Index	Volatility	Multiple of Consumer Price Index	Multiple of Industrial Product Price Index
	(1)	(2)	(3)
Agricultural	10.6	11.8	7.9
Forestry	4.8	5.3	3.5
Energy	5.4	6.3	4.0
Metals	5.1	6.0	3.9
Aggregate Primary Product Index	3.6	4.0	0.7
Consumer Price Index	0.9	–	0.7
Industrial Product Price Index	1.3	1.5	–

Note: Column 2 is derived by dividing column 1 by the measure of the volatility of the Consumer Price Index; column 3 is derived by dividing column 2 by the measure of the volatility of the Industrial Product Price Index.

Sources: Commodity price index coefficients from price series constructed at the Western Centre for Economic Research, University of Alberta, Edmonton; Consumer Price Index and Industrial Product Price Index coefficients from Statistics Canada.

data for the Consumer Price Index and the Industrial Product Price Index. Since these coefficients are based on quarterly percentage rates of price change rather than on levels of prices, a direct comparison based on standard deviations is possible. The outstanding feature of this table is the high degree of price variability of the West's main exports. On the other hand, import prices, as proxied by the Industrial Product Price Index, are only slightly more variable than consumer prices.

Variability in Economic Aggregates

Figures 2, 3 and 4 show the variability of GDP, total and per capita personal income, and population, respectively, for all ten provinces and the whole of Canada. Regardless of which measure is used, the Western provinces — except Manitoba — demonstrate a much greater level of economic variability than do the other provinces or

Figure 2:   *The Variability of Provincial GDP, 1961–85*

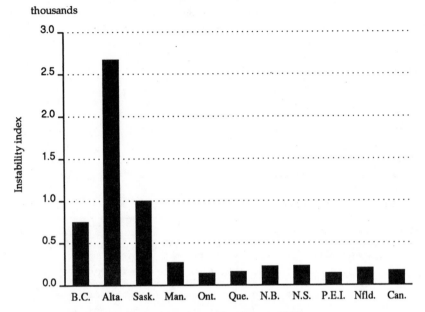

Note: The value for the Yukon and Northwest Territories is 4,667.

Source: Robert L. Mansell and Michael B. Percy, *Strength in Adversity: A Study of the Alberta Economy*, Western Studies in Economic Policy 1 (Edmonton: University of Alberta Press for the Western Centre for Economic Research, 1990), p. 72.

national average. This is due, in part, to the price variability noted previously; it also stems from movements in the exchange rate.

A New Way to Measure the Real Exchange Rate

In the post-1973 period, following the international economy's adoption of a floating exchange-rate regime, volatility in the external value of the Canadian dollar has contributed to the commodity price volatility facing Western Canadian producers. Variations in the external value of the dollar can offset fluctuations in commodity prices in two ways. First, if the external value of the dollar appreciates when

Figure 3: *The Variability of Total Personal Income and Per Capita Personal Income by Province, 1961–85*

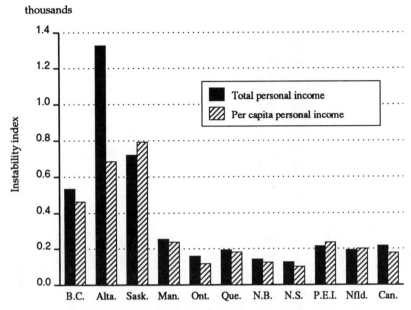

Note: For the Yukon and Northwest Territories the value of total personal income is 336; the value of per capita personal income is 329.

Source: Robert L. Mansell and Michael B. Percy, *Strength in Adversity: A Study of the Alberta Economy*, Western Studies in Economic Policy 1 (Edmonton: University of Alberta Press for the Western Centre for Economic Research, 1990), p. 72.

commodity prices are rising, this can temper the stimulus to economic activity, while a depreciation when prices are falling can counter the pressure on producers' profit margins. Second, currency changes can have perverse effects on producers if appreciation accompanies commodity price declines and depreciation accompanies commodity price increases. The Western Centre for Economic Research (WCER) has designed a new exchange-rate index to take these variations into account.[5] Its principal features are that it reflects

---

5 For more detail, see E.J. Chambers, "Indexes of Effective Exchange Rates for Western Canada," Information Bulletin 2 (Edmonton: Western Centre for Economic Research, 1991).

Figure 4: *The Variability of*
Population by Province, 1961–85

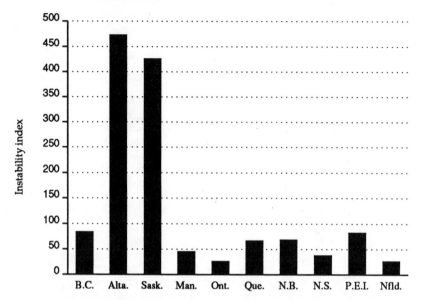

Note: The value for the Yukon and Northwest Territories is 1,389.

Source: Robert L. Mansell and Michael B. Percy, *Strength in Adversity: A Study of the Alberta Economy*, Western Studies in Economic Policy 1 (Edmonton: University of Alberta Press for the Western Centre for Economic Research, 1990), p. 74.

the importance of Western Canada's leading export commodities and their destinations, and it is double weighted to take into account third-country competition.

The evidence from the two existing exchange-rate indexes — the Bank of Canada's index of the Group-of-Seven industrial countries and that of WCER — indicates that exchange-rate movements did move perversely for part of the period in question — the second quarter of 1972 to the fourth quarter of 1988 — in that they tended to amplify booms and exacerbate contractions in Western Canada through reinforcing commodity price movements.

Regression analysis — using the quarterly percentage rate of change of employment in Western Canada as the dependent variable, and the quarterly percentage change in real commodity prices and the index of real effective exchange rates as the two independent variables, with one- and two-quarter lags — confirms the important effect of both variables. The cumulative effect of a 1 percent rise in commodity prices over three quarters is a 0.2 percent increase in employment, while an increase in the real exchange rate of 1 percent is associated with a 0.3 percent decline in employment.[6]

Mechanisms of Interregional Adjustment

The provinces and regions of Canada trade with one another on a fixed exchange rate — the Canadian dollar. Hence, the provincial economies adjust to terms-of-trade shocks and other economic disturbances through several mechanisms, of which relative price movements and migration are the most important — at least in the short to medium run. The price movements of interest concern the way in which traded prices vary relative to nontrade prices — in other words, the relative price of traded goods. When a regional economy is in decline, nontraded prices — of which housing is perhaps the most visible — often decline compared with traded prices, and this shift in relative prices helps improve the competitive position of the region in external markets. Conversely, booming regions often experience rapidly rising nontraded prices compared with traded ones. This shift in relative prices helps ameliorate the magnitude of the boom and to bring the regional balance of payments into equilibrium.

As a proxy for nontraded prices, one can use land prices. These will change for many reasons directly unrelated to adjustment issues — for example, changes in property taxes. Nonetheless, it is likely that overall variability, as shown by Figures 2, 3, and 4, and the traded-price volatility illustrated in Table 6, will be reflected in land

---

6 See Chambers and Percy, *Western Canada in the International Economy*.

Table 7:   Volatility of Land Prices, Selected Cities, 1976–87
(as measured by the standard
deviation of annual percentage change)

	Volatility
Toronto	4.57
Winnipeg	4.78
Regina	4.18
Edmonton	10.44
Vancouver	16.14
Canada average	*4.80*

Sources: Statistics Canada, *Construction Price Statistics*, Cat. no. 62-007; and idem, *Industry Price Indexes*, CANSIM.

prices. The evidence on the volatility of land prices for selected cities is given in Table 7, which shows that prices in Vancouver and Edmonton are significantly more volatile than those in Toronto or Canada as a whole. Surprisingly, land prices are slightly less volatile in Winnipeg or Regina than the Canadian average.

Regional economies are not immune from the phenomenon of the "Dutch disease", where deindustrialization accompanies resource booms. In national economies, an appreciating exchange rate during periods of rising resource prices squeezes the competitive position of traditional (nonresource) export industries and domestic import-competing goods industries. For regional economies, movements in nontraded prices perform much the same role. Escalating nontraded prices also hinder the competitive position of traditional export industries and import-competing goods industries during resource booms. Conversely, during slumps in resource prices, nontraded prices might fall disproportionately. However, the incentives for industrialization or greater diversification are often offset by high rates of out-migration and declining domestic demand.

An additional problem faced by resource-rich Western Canadian economies is that government revenues often move in synchronization with resource prices, especially in Alberta and Saskatchewan. Hence, government fiscal policy may tend to exacerbate swings in market-induced activity initiated by resource-price movements.

Real fixed capital formation by the public and private sectors in Western Canada during the 1972–88 period was almost twice as volatile (9.65 percent compared with 5.44 percent) as that for Canada. For the rest of Canada excluding the West, the contrast is even greater (9.65 percent compared with 4.90 percent). It is clear that the volatility of resource prices is reflected in the volatility of fixed capital formation in the West, particularly in Alberta. This arises from three main sources. The first is the volatility of resource prices and the capital-intensive nature of investments in the sector. The second is the response of interregional migration to resource-price movements and the shifts this tends to induce in population-sensitive capital formation — such as in the housing sector. The third is the sensitivity of provincial government capital formation to provincial resource revenues, which, in turn, are themselves volatile.

The evidence for the West as whole also indicates that interregional migration is an important mechanism of adjustment. Table 8 provides estimates of the contribution of net migration to population change for regions and provinces. On the margin, net migration appears to be a more significant component of population change for the West than for other regions or provinces. The alternative to interregional migration as a response to changes in regional economic activity is greater variability in income or unemployment.

Implications for Alternate Constitutional Scenarios

As noted earlier, Western Canada's two most important sources of economic gain from Confederation are (i) market power in international markets and (ii) regional economic stabilization and risk pooling. With that in mind, what do the data imply for Western Canada under three alternative constitutional scenarios: the status quo, a revitalized Confederation, and an independent Western Canada?

Table 8:   ***Contribution of Migration to Regional Population***
              Change in Canada, 1985 and 1989
              (percent)

Region	1985	1989
Western Canada	–38.8%	13.8%
Ontario	28.6	–4.3
Quebec	–7.9	–14.3
Atlantic Canada	–5.3	7.2

Sources: Statistics Canada, *Report on the Demographic Situation in Canada*, Cat. no. 91-209; and
          idem, *Interprovincial Migration*, Cat. no. 91-001.

Market Power in Trade

In the case of market power, there really is no distinction between
the status quo and a revitalized Confederation. Rather, the question
here is: Would the West fare better as an independent entity or as
part of the Canadian economic union?

The Western Canadian economy is highly specialized in a narrow range of resource and processed-resource products destined for
a geographically concentrated set of international markets. Had the
West been an independent entity in 1986, it is highly likely that the
softwood lumber dispute with the United States would have ended
with that country imposing a countervailing duty and the revenues
accruing to the U.S. Treasury. The actual outcome — an export tax
levied by the federal government as an interim measure until the
provinces modified their timber-pricing systems — probably reflects
in no small measure the greater market power that a larger economy
has in resolving trade disputes. A similar argument could be made
in the potash antidumping case. The outcome was unfavorable from
Saskatchewan's perspective, but it was probably better than would
have been the case for an independent Western Canada.

Because of its pattern of trade and industrial structure, Western
Canada is extremely vulnerable to the costs of U.S. protectionism.
Successful countervail and antidumping suits brought by U.S. pro-
ducers will be at the expense of resource producers in the West and

those governments and people whose incomes derive from these sectors. The potential for Western Canadian resource producers successfully to withstand the exercise of monopsony power by the United States or other countries is greater within an economic union than it is outside. Trade harassment will continue, but the costs would be less for the West within the economic union than on its own.

The current discussions under the Canada-U.S. FTA on a common definition of subsidy, if successful, will probably lead to a more favorable definition from the perspective of Western Canada than the region as a separate entity could negotiate. Moreover, it is by no means clear that a separate Western Canada could be a party to the current FTA. Indeed, it is unlikely that the FTA would remain intact if Canada were to fragment.[7] While the various Canadian regions would hope the Agreement would remain in force, this outcome is by no means in the United States' best interests nor perhaps is it consistent with the enabling legislation for the Agreement.

Insurance and Stabilization Issues

By almost any measure, Western Canada is a highly volatile economy because of its industrial structure, specialization in products exhibiting significant price volatility, and concentration in a few export markets. It is reflected in a range of macroeconomic variables and in mechanisms of adjustment such as shifts in relative prices within the region and interregional migration.

Which of the constitutional scenarios best deals with this characteristic of the Western Canadian economy? A stand-alone economy would likely exhibit even greater volatility than it does under the status quo and certainly more than a revitalized Confederation with policy instruments directed specifically at insurance and stabilization issues. If it were independent, the West would be barred from

---

7 This argument is explored in Richard G. Lipsey, "Trade Issues Involved in Quebec 'Separation'" (Paper presented at the Meeting of Western Economists on the Constitution, Simon Fraser Harbour Centre, Vancouver, March 20–21, 1991).

many current avenues of interregional adjustment to economic shocks.[8] Shifts in real income and wages, rather than adjustments through interregional migration and asset transfers through the national banking system, would become the dominant mechanism of adjustment. Income and unemployment variability would necessarily be greater in an independent West than they are now.

Although we noted earlier that exchange-rate movements tend to exacerbate swings in economic activity in the West, it is not clear that control over the exchange rate would reduce economic volatility. Just the reverse might be true. The Canadian dollar currently reflects trade flows and relative prices of traded goods from all regions of the country. Price shocks for any one commodity, such as energy, accordingly have less effect on the exchange rate. Were the West to stand alone and have its own currency, movements in the new currency would be dominated by a few commodities characterized by a high degree of volatility. The region could adopt a fixed exchange rate or use the U.S. dollar as its currency, but this would shift the mechanism of adjustment to balance-of-payments shocks from the exchange rate to movements in relative prices in the Western Canadian economy. Nontraded prices and their movement relative to traded prices would play a more important role in how the domestic economy accommodated balance-of-payment disturbances.

Perhaps more importantly, the West would no longer be able to pool risks nationally, since Canada's industrial structure is more diversified than that of any one region. An independent West would be much less able to provide economic stabilization than does the present Canadian federation because it would no longer have as diversified a tax base on which to draw.

Although the institutional framework of Confederation does not deal well with Western Canadian economic volatility, that does not mean a revitalized Confederation could not address the problem. Designing unemployment insurance programs that were truly in-

---

8 See Thomas J. Courchene, "Avenues of Adjustment: The Transfer System and Regional Disparities," in *Canadian Confederation at the Crossroads: The Search for a Federal-Provincial Balance* (Vancouver: Fraser Institute, 1978).

surance programs, rather than income-maintenance schemes for declining regions and sectors, would be an integral part of the reform. Ensuring that federal transfer programs were automatically more responsive to cyclical regional economic conditions and less directed to preserving the spatial distribution of population regardless of long-run economic prospects would also be required. Federal policies that promoted labor mobility and more efficient, market-based regional adjustment mechanisms would further enhance the insurance/stabilization aspects of the economic union. Much of the institutional infrastructure underlying federal-provincial fiscal relations now seems directed to dissipating whatever economic surplus might exist from the economic union.

Issues of Regional Equity

A revitalized economic union would also have to address the issue of the distribution of the potential economic surplus. A study undertaken for the Macdonald Royal Commission in 1986 indicated that the structure of Confederation generated a negative economic surplus and discriminated significantly against resource-producing regions.[9] While the study's conclusions reflect its choice of a 1981 base year and the distortions introduced into the energy sector by the since-dismantled National Energy Program, an array of federal policies continue to dissipate portions (or all) of the gains from the economic union.

Data available on regional net fiscal balances — federal revenues in a province minus disbursements — also indicate that, on equity and insurance grounds, one can fault federal policies, especially in their effects on the Alberta and British Columbia economies.[10] Shifting the focus of the institutions of Confederation from

9 John Whalley and Irene Trela, *Regional Aspects of Confederation*, Collected Research Studies of the Royal Commission on the Economic Union and Development Prospects for Canada 68 (Toronto: University of Toronto Press, 1986).

10 See Robert L. Mansell and R.C. Schlenker, "An Analysis of the Regional Distribution of Federal Fiscal Balances: An Update," Department of Economics Research Paper (Calgary: University of Calgary, 1990).

maintaining the status quo in the spatial distribution of economic activity and population in Canada to dealing with the consequences of economic volatility would improve the well-being of all residents of Canada, not just those in Western Canada, and would contribute to increasing the surplus of the economic union.

It should be noted that the West has been a beneficiary of federal transfers, especially to the grains and transportation sector. One might well question whether continued large-scale transfers to the grains industry are in the best interests of the region or the country if they delay the industry's adjustment to a far more competitive international trading environment.

The Political Economy of Resource Specialization

Suppose Western Canada, with its resource-dependent economy, were to become a sovereign nation. What kind of government would emerge? Would the West be a federal or a unitary state? What role would government play in the economy? Would it be *laissez-faire* or interventionist in its approach to the market?

Fiscal Relations in Western Canada

Because remaining Dominion Lands in Western Canada were transferred to provincial jurisdiction as late as 1930, Crown ownership of the resource base in the West is significant and the transfer of ownership to the private sector has not occurred to the same extent as in the rest of Canada. There are considerable differences among the Western provinces in revenues captured by government from the resource base, although the magnitude of potential rents today are likely nowhere near as high as estimated by the Economic Council of Canada in 1980, when real energy prices were far higher.

In a recent study, economist R.S. Smith provides estimates of resource revenues captured by provincial (and local) governments in the West on a per capita basis.[11] Substantial variations exist in the level of these revenues for a given province through time and across provinces at a point in time. Alberta has the highest level of per capita resource revenues captured by government, with a significant gap between it and Saskatchewan. Next comes British Columbia, with Manitoba falling well below it.

In fiscal year 1982/83, the Alberta government had per capita natural resource revenues of $2,049 in constant (1981) dollars. The corresponding figure had fallen to $805 by 1987/88. Manitoba, on the other hand, had per capita resource revenues of $33 in 1982/83 and $42 in 1987/88. By comparison, the Ontario provincial government had per capita resource revenues of $14 and $21 in 1982/83 and 1987/88, respectively.

Smith also estimates the tax effort and tax capacity for Canadian provinces in 1988. These data show that variations between tax effort and capacity for the Western provinces are significant. The design of a stand-alone Western regional grouping would, with current provincial configurations, face the same problems that now confound the federal government, with equalization payments, Established Programs Financing, and the Canada Assistance Plan.

A substantial body of literature demonstrates that interprovincial migration is responsive to fiscal incentives and argues that such migration is inefficient. It is clear that net fiscal benefits related to location can influence both interregional and intraregional migration. A central government in an independent West would have to deal with incentives generated by net fiscal benefits that differed from one province to another and would have to introduce some form of equalization if the provinces to remain as separate entities.

The evidence suggests that only a unitary state would make sense in an independent West. The alternative — the existing configuration of provinces and a Western central government with a significant redistributive role — would be an institutional structure

---

11 R.S. Smith, "Spending and Taxing: The Recent Record of Western Canadian Provincial Governments," *Information Bulletin* 1 (Edmonton: Western Centre for Economic Research, 1990).

that would cost much to maintain given the region's relatively small population base. It would be unrealistic to presume that Westerners would want to replicate a central government with many of the Canadian federal government's functions but on a smaller economic base.

The Role of Government in an Independent West

In 1988, a random sample of 1,145 Albertans was asked the following question:

> Some claim that economic specialization in Alberta is *desirable* because it is efficient and leads to higher income. Others argue that specialization in Alberta is *not desirable* because incomes and employment, while higher on average, are less stable. Which view do you agree with?

Of the 1,045 respondents who had an opinion, 26.48 percent said that economic specialization was desirable, while 73.52 percent said it was not.[12] Surprisingly, perhaps, neither place of residence — that is, urban versus rural — nor educational attainment are sufficient to account for individuals' responses to the question. Those employed in nontraded industries or who were burdened with mortgage payments did, however, tend to view specialization as undesirable.

The strong preference for a less-specialized economy in response to this and other questions in the survey suggests considerable support of diversification strategies even though such policies would have a negative effect on incomes. Since a *laissez-faire* Western Canadian economy likely would become even more specialized and more volatile than it is now, it is highly possible that the political marketplace would lead Western politicians to be highly interventionist in the regional economy. Thus, any set of policies that would further enhance the market incentives for greater specialization or increase the degree of regional economic instability would undoubt-

---

12 For details on this survey, see Mansell and Percy, *Strength in Adversity*.

edly lead to the demand for provincial diversification policies —
with all their associated economic inefficiencies.

Conclusion

Two basic themes emerge from this analysis. First, continued economic specialization by the West in natural resource products (inclu-
sive of agriculture) has important implications for trade policy,
elements of fiscal federalism, and regional adjustment issues, especially those concerning the labor market. Resource markets do differ
in some respects from markets for services and secondary manufactured products, and they influence the likelihood of trade disputes,
the variability of the Western Canadian economy, mechanisms of
regional adjustment to economic shocks, and how residents view the
operation of market forces.

Second, despite the importance of the natural resources and
agricultural sectors in Western Canada, there is significant economic
diversity among the four provinces. These intraregional differences
are probably sufficiently large that many of the problems that currently confound federal-provincial relations would remain and perhaps be even more serious for an independent Western Canada.

A Comment

Dane Rowlands

Ted Chambers and Mike Percy provide an interesting and data-intensive analysis of the "Western Canadian" economy. They argue that the resource-based Western Canadian economy is exceptionally volatile, and that a Canadian economic union provides at least the opportunity for stabilization. Not only are resource industries inherently unstable — a proposition with an ancient pedigree in the economic development literature — but they are also most vulnerable to international trade disputes. While the authors may offer some encouragement to those of us who would like to see Canada remain united, they also leave us with the challenge of how to realize the potential of providing stability to the four Western provinces.

Chambers and Percy begin with a framework — attributed to Judith Maxwell and Caroline Pestieau — identifying the sources of potential gain in an economic union. Of the four identified sources — specialization, shared fixed costs of overhead, risk diversification, and market power — the authors concentrate on the latter two. In this sense, they are unusually forward looking, and manage to get away from the traditional discussion of how tariffs were used to distort the specialization of the regional economies. It would be interesting, however, to hear their views on the national tariff system, since some of the distortions that generated the current economic structure are probably still in existence. It might have been useful if the authors had identified the policies they would like to see changed in this regard. I think, however, that they quite correctly focus on how the economic union can deal with the current problems Western Canada faces, and not on how the economic union has affected the regional economy over the past century.

Chambers and Percy spend the most time discussing the instability of the Western Canadian economy and providing measures of economic instability. While I am sympathetic to the idea of instability being a common feature of primary-producing economies, some of the data that the authors present require further refinement and explanation for those of us who are unfamiliar with the region's economy. It is not clear to me that the trend in some of these variables has been adequately accounted for — for example, a series demonstrating high but constant growth over a long period of time will exhibit a large standard deviation. It is also possible that instability in one series might be offset by variations in another. In Table 6, for example, the lower standard deviation of the Aggregate Primary Product Index is less than that of the four component indices listed. Since primary product prices exhibit similarities in their cycles, refining the data to account for trend and providing cross-series correlations might strengthen the authors' arguments.

The degree to which income instability in Western Canada is correlated with income movements in the rest of Canada is critical to the proposition that Confederation can create a mechanism to provide interregional insurance. If Central Canadian incomes are falling at the same time as those in the West, then the opportunity for insurance is dramatically reduced relative to the case where income movements are in opposite directions. Chambers and Percy therefore highlight an area for additional research concerning the magnitude of the potential insurance gains.

These potential gains are unlikely to be realized, however, if governments are as myopic as Chambers and Percy suggest they are in the section on fiscal policy. With revenues being closely correlated with the strength of the resource sector, provincial governments in Western Canada have experienced dramatic fluctuations in their fiscal capacity. The authors state that these fiscal cycles reinforce the movements in the economy, making good times better and bad times worse. While those people who looked at Alberta's Heritage Fund with envy may be surprised at the inability of provincial governments to smooth out their expenditure — or even to engage in countercyclical stabilization policies — the evidence suggests that the myopia of governments cannot be overestimated. If a provincial government is unable or unwilling to insure itself against revenue volatility, it does not seem likely that such a scheme would work well between provinces.

The discussion about interregional adjustment through currency changes, migration, and relative price changes is a very good one, although the discussion of a separate currency for the West could have been more elaborate. Chambers and Percy provide evidence of the destabilizing effect of currency movements within Canada. This evidence might lend support to the idea that a separate currency in a separate Western Canada could be beneficial to the region. A more thorough discussion of the pros and cons of a separate currency, perhaps within the context of an optimal currency area, would have been interesting.

Population instability is a major concern of the authors. They emphasize the importance of labor mobility in the process of interregional equilibration, and argue that migration flows are volatile and, therefore, likely to be very responsive to employment conditions. The statistics that Chambers and Percy present are startling to anyone writing from the perspective of Atlantic Canada, where extensive out-migration is considered a social scourge that is, in some sense, unique to the region.[1] There are probably subtle differences in form, however, between Western and Eastern migration. Atlantic Canadians worry because of a drain of skilled workers to Central Canada, with most in- and out-migration probably due to movements of Atlantic Canadians in both directions. A Western Canadian regionalist might not be too upset about volatile populations if the migrating components of the population were Central or Atlantic Canadians. While further research on exactly who is migrating is obviously needed, Chambers and Percy make it clear that

---

1 Most of us are aware of the high degree of out-migration from the poorer regions of the West, such as Saskatchewan. The concern over out-migration probably has a longer tradition in the Atlantic provinces, however, and the experience of Saskatchewan is of more recent vintage and attributable more clearly to cycles of boom and bust rather than to steady decline.

migration is at least as important a phenomenon in Western Canada as it is in Atlantic Canada, and some Atlantic Canadian "myths" about migration do seem to be in need of reformulation in the light of more sophisticated data.

The discussion of market power is very good, and certainly seems more realistic than some previous commentary. The reports for Quebec's Bélanger-Campeau Commission, in particular, seem to be too optimistic about the possibility of maintaining current trading agreements and arrangements. Other Canadians should not take comfort in this, since, as Chambers and Percy suggest, all regions of the country would be more vulnerable to international pressure if Canada dissolved.

Atlantic Canadians will likely welcome the view that insurance should be provided across, rather than within, regions. A move to regionalize unemployment insurance — as the Quebec government has indicated it might prefer — would be extremely detrimental to Atlantic Canada. The arguments of Chambers and Percy provide little comfort for Atlantic Canadians, however, since they are concerned with the insurance portion of the interregional financial flows, not the transfer element. They identify what may well be the fundamental conflict between Atlantic Canadians and Western Canadians with respect to the Constitution: How much of the current effort to support the "status quo in the spatial distribution of economic activity and population" is to be diverted to other endeavors, such as dealing with economic volatility? The principles of economic efficiency and the free market seem to have been embraced more firmly in the West than in the Atlantic provinces, where there seems to be greater concern for equity, and economic and cultural survival.

Chambers and Percy ask one of the most important questions: Is Confederation worth the effort? They cite the study by John Whalley and Irene Trela for the Macdonald Commission, which suggests that Confederation has generated a negative economic surplus. It would be useful to see the gains and losses for each region, since British Columbia and Alberta — along with Ontario — are usually considered to be major financial contributors to Confederation. The data might suggest that Western Canada has signed up for an extremely expensive insurance scheme. Chambers and Percy present survey data that demonstrate risk aversion, but they do not tell us how much Western Canadians are willing to pay to reduce risk.

In conclusion, I am relieved that Chambers and Percy have come up with convincing arguments in favor of renewed federalism. They have demonstrated the volatility of the Western Canadian economy and have linked it to that region's dependence on natural resources. This volatility presents Canada with the opportunity to smooth out regional cycles with national programs. The discussion of market power in the international context highlights another source of economic benefit that might be derived from continued economic union. Western Canadians and Atlantic Canadians might differ with respect to how much income is to be transferred across regions and how freely economic adjustment mechanisms are to be permitted to function. However, the exploitation of risk-diversifying opportunities and international market power — which Chambers and Percy identify as the chief sources of economic gain to be had from federalism — are compatible or coincident with Atlantic Canadian economic welfare as well. My only concern is that the strength of their pro-federalist argument lies in the potential for gains in the future, rather than on any gains that we have demonstrated an ability to exploit in the past.

The View from the Less-Affluent West

Norman Cameron, Derek Hum, and Wayne Simpson

In the foreword to the report of the Citizens' Forum on Canada's Future, Keith Spicer proclaimed bluntly: "When all is said and done, Canada is a breath-taking challenge of perspective — perspective of mind and heart. You can try to find this in Rimouski or Weyburn."[1] Mention of these two towns recalls not only the Central Canadian issue of reconciling French-speaking and English-speaking communities but also present Western attitudes toward Quebec, particularly the attitude of the less-affluent West symbolized by Weyburn to those distant relatives in rural Quebec symbolized by Rimouski. The latter are known to exist by report, but there has been virtually no contact with them for as long as one can remember. Western members of the family often seem more preoccupied with the fortunes of that nearer and richer brother, Ontario.

Does a distinctly different set of concerns about Canada's constitutional future spring from the less-affluent and less-populous part of the West, from Manitoba and Saskatchewan? We suggest that there are some subtle differences between these two provinces' perspectives and those of the undifferentiated West. We do not believe these differences are merely the result of what economists call "different tastes"; neither do we believe they are a matter of accident or whim. The starting point for our comments is that the

---

1 Canada, Citizens' Forum on Canada's Future, *Report* (Ottawa: Supply and Services Canada, 1991), p. 1.

unique Manitoba and Saskatchewan perspective is partly attributable to the peculiar economic and social situation of the two provinces relative to the rest of Canada and even to the rest of the West.
Accordingly, we first sketch those material and cultural facts about
the situation of each province that seem to condition constitutional
perspectives. Next, we discuss the constitutional perspectives these
conditions cause. Finally, we conclude with some personal and
scientifically untestable observations.[2]

The Less-Affluent West: Some Facts

Table 1 provides some salient facts about the economic and political
strength of Manitoba and Saskatchewan; also presented, as a bench-
mark, is Ontario, the province once proposed officially as the standard for equalization.[3]

The statistics need little commentary. Manitoba and Saskatchewan are less thickly settled and less urbanized than Ontario. They
command fewer parliamentary seats than that province. Manitoba
and Saskatchewan are net exporters of people, while Ontario is a net
recipient. Both Western provinces have much higher concentrations
of specific non-British and non-French ethnic groups than does
Ontario. The common perception of Ontario as a concentration of
manufacturing activity while Saskatchewan is more heavily involved in the primary sector is well borne out by output statistics;
Manitoba is somewhere between the two.

These facts have helped shape political circumstances and attitudes in the less-affluent West. Because they have populations that
are tiny compared with the national total, Manitoba and Saskatchewan do not, even together, have much influence on national policy
by weight of political representatives. There is no prospect of this

---

2 Of the three authors, only Wayne Simpson is a native of the two provinces whose
  perspective is discussed in this paper. Norman Cameron is from Ontario and Derek
  Hum is from the Maritimes, although both are now naturalized Manitobans.

3 Further details on the economic structure of all four Western provinces, are
  provided by E.J. Chambers and M.B. Percy in this volume.

Table 1: *Major Characteristics of Manitoba, Saskatchewan, and Ontario*

	Manitoba	Saskatchewan	Ontario
Population (% of Canadian total, 1988)[a]	4.19	3.90	36.38
Area (% of Canadian total)[a]	5.95	6.19	9.67
Members of Parliament[a]	14	14	99
Urban population (% of total)[b]	72.1	61.4	82.6
Interprovincial migration (% of population)[c]			
Average net flow, 1970–89	−0.51	−0.68	0.11
Maximum net inflow	0.15 (1982)	0.71 (1975)	0.71 (1970)
Minimum net inflow	−1.35 (1979)	−3.06 (1970)	−0.30 (1975)
Major ethnic groups (% of total population)[a]			
British/British and other	58.10	49.43	59.99
French/French and other	10.98	8.73	12.75
German only	9.16	12.93	3.17
Ukrainian only	7.62	6.08	1.22
Italian only	0.78	0.20	5.13
Output shares[d]			
Primary	10.8	24.6	5.2
Secondary	18.4	12.8	29.0
Services	70.8	62.6	65.0
Primary output shares[d]			
Agriculture	50.0	55.0	22.5
Other primary	19.0	34.0	27.4
Utilities	31.0	11.0	50.1
Manufacturing shares[e, f, g]			
Food processing	17.5	19.2	12.1
Transportation equipment	12.8	2.2	17.0
Clothing	8.6	0.7	3.0
Fabricated metal	7.1	9.9	8.0
Printing and publishing	9.9	n.a.	6.1
Electrical and electronic	5.9	8.3	8.0
Primary metals	5.7	n.a.	8.0

Sources:

[a] Statistics Canada, *Canada Year Book 1990*, Cat. no. 11-402.

[b] Statistics Canada, Census 1986, Focus on Canada, *Canada's Population from Ocean to Ocean*, Cat. no. 98-120.

[c] Statistics Canada, *Report on the Demographic Situation in Canada 1990*, Cat no. 91-209.

[d] Conference Board of Canada, 1991; figures made available by Manitoba, Department of Finance.

[e] Manitoba, *Statistical Review*, 4th quarter, 1990.

[f] Saskatchewan, Bureau of Statistics, *Economic Review*, 43 (1989).

[g] Ontario, Ministry of Treasury and Economics, *Ontario Statistics 1986*.

situation changing in the foreseeable future,1 since both provinces have experienced net outmigration in most years since 1973.

Saskatchewan is predominantly rural. Manitoba is as urban as the national average, but two-thirds of the population live in or very close to Winnipeg, which is the location of almost all of the province's manufacturing. In other words, Manitoba is virtually a one-city province. (In this sense, Manitoba is more "East" than "West".)

The rural sectors of both provinces depend on a handful of primary products. Wheat and potash in Saskatchewan, wheat and nickel in Manitoba dominate the output figures for goods. Of these, wheat is sold into an international market in which the individual Canadian producer is relatively small. Potash and nickel are also sold into international markets, but the Canadian producers are fairly large. In other words, rural Manitoba and Saskatchewan are still staples-based economies, but there is just a hint of market power potential if only external demand would materialize substantially and securely.

Like Ontario and Quebec and unlike other Western provinces, Manitoba has a large and fairly diversified manufacturing sector. It consists of many small to medium-size firms in each industry (rather than a few large household names, like those of the Ontario motor vehicles industry). Some of this secondary sector is in food-processing of some sort and therefore tied to agriculture, but much is not. Saskatchewan, on the other hand, depends heavily on its primary sector and on a dominant product — wheat. (In this way, Saskatchewan is much like Alberta, with steadily low-priced wheat substituted for unpredictably low-priced oil.) In comparison, Manitoba's primary sector is much less important in the province's economy. It is also much more diversified, being divided roughly into quarters of cereals farming, livestock farming, other primary output (mainly mining), and utilities (mainly hydro-electric power). The result is a more stable level of total output growth in Manitoba than in Saskatchewan. The standard deviation of annual output growth since 1962 has been 4.0 percent in Manitoba but 9.5 percent in Saskatchewan (compared with 3.0 percent in Ontario and 8.1 percent in

Alberta). It is often said that Manitoba's growth is "slow but steady" in bad times and "steady but slow" in good. The fortunes of Saskatchewan are tied to the price of wheat, an internationally determined matter. Consequently, the two provinces have quite different needs for safety nets and stabilization policy.

Since their founding, both Manitoba and Saskatchewan have had a rich mix of ethnic groups, including a large number of native Canadians and Métis, on and off reserves. Neither province has as dominant a majority group as that which people of French origin represent in Quebec or that which people of British origin represent in the Maritimes. Each has a population block of Ukrainian and German origin large enough to make its mainstream less Anglo-Saxon than Ontario's.

The sense of distance between the less-affluent West and Central Canada is both physical and cultural. In kilometres and in air flight time, Manitoba and Saskatchewan are a long way from Central Canada. Although many Manitobans can identify with Kenora and some even with Thunder Bay, few can stretch to Sault Ste. Marie or Sudbury, let alone to Toronto. The concerns of Quebec seem even more remote, being blocked not only by the greater physical distance but also by unfamiliar language, cultural differences, and lack of close encounters of any kind. The concerns of Quebec may have a large indirect effect, but the people of Manitoba and Saskatchewan seem to perceive little direct impact from southern Ontario, let alone from Quebec.

Finally, a word about the political culture of the less-affluent West. The two provinces' marginal status has undoubtedly contributed to their political traditions. Manitoba sees itself as centralist and constructive, favoring a strong national government, understanding and appreciating federal spending power, concerned with fairness from Ottawa, and modestly confident that it can measure up to national performance norms in selected niches. It is firmly in the middle, at the extremes of neither the political right nor left wing, Eastern nor Western cultural identification, rich nor poor economy. Saskatchewan is more populist in orientation, believing in locally generated solutions and cooperative help for reasons of social insurance rather than redistribution. Its radicalism is born more out of the reciprocal aid relationships thought necessary in the face of hostile nature than an inequitable social structure. It also appreciates federal fiscal support, especially in agriculture, which it feels is too often accorded something between total neglect and grudging attention.

Constitutional Perspectives

The constitutional perspectives of the less-affluent West seem usefully grouped by three objectives that it wishes to see achieved — or at least protected — by a constitution: political equality, economic equity, and efficiency. All regions of Canada also have these objectives, and each of them can be achieved by a variety of means. But different means elicit different reactions in different parts of country. We mention here those on which Manitoba and Saskatchewan have specific reactions.

Political Equality

As provinces with small populations, Manitoba and Saskatchewan feel marginalized in the national political system, in which power ultimately is parceled out by the principle of representation by population. Their representation, it is feared, will never be strong enough to guarantee national support for provincial objectives, and their federal representatives frequently complain about that lack. This reaction might be simply the paranoia of the ungrateful and the forgetful, but abandonment of rail lines in Saskatchewan and of the port of Churchill in Manitoba are cases in point that continue to add to the political conditioning and skepticism of Westerners. The proposal for a Triple-E Senate plays to these feelings, and the West has aggressively seized it as an institutional solution. The fact that the Western provinces have often elected New Democratic Party governments while the federal government has always been in the hands of one of the other mainline parties emphasizes the gap between the West and Ottawa.

Since none of the ethnic groups so prominent in Manitoba and Saskatchewan sees itself as a dominant majority, each individual is a member of a minority. Thus, all are greatly interested in the protection of individual rights through the Charter of Rights and Freedoms. No group wants to see these rights infringed on to benefit the majority (as Quebec's language legislation is thought to do in protecting its francophones' culture); each group can visualize itself as a potential victim. There is, therefore, little support for Quebec's wish to be somehow above the Charter, as through distinct society phrasing or unrestrained use of the notwithstanding clause with political impunity. Manitoba's enthusiasm for greater concern for protection of individual rights is shown in its legislation to disallow discrimination on the basis of age; this goes further than the national Charter. Manitoba's opposition to the Meech Lake Accord is perhaps more a reflection of worry about the dangers of the distinct society clause than about provincial checks on the federal spending power.

Economic Equity

Saskatchewan and Manitoba are concerned about having the rest of Canada as a safety valve to absorb excess additions to the labor force in bad years (to avoid having to lower wage increases to clear the labor market) and to supply labor in fat years.[4] The pattern of migration to and from both provinces shows that this safety valve has been used there much more than in Ontario. Any further fragmentation of the Canadian common market for labor would make the cyclical swings of the less-affluent West more painful.

Both provinces are strongly concerned about equality of opportunity for their residents, though the concept means different things in each province. In Manitoba, with a better-diversified economy and a wide range of outputs to sell, it means fair internal markets in Canada. The awarding of the CF-18 contract to Montreal was a

---

4 Both are less concerned than volatile Alberta, however. See the discussion and tables in E.J. Chambers and M.B. Percy in this volume on the variability of population, income, output, and prices across all provinces.

flagrant violation of what Manitobans regard as fundamental fairness by the very agency on which Manitobans must rely to ensure fairness elsewhere. This decision was seen as illustrating the perfidy of Ottawa in both economic judgment and fundamental fair play. Worse, it confirmed all Western fears that Quebec holds both the upper hand and the favored outstretched palm in regional economic patronage. The CF-18 episode is destined for Western Canada history books as the supreme metaphor of Western economic competence trumped by Quebec's special status. The incident still rankles.

Saskatchewan is focused on international grain markets more than on any internal market. It expects the federal government to represent its interests internationally in combating unfair dumping by the European Community and the United States. It feels that if Ontario had a commodity or sector — beer, for example? — as significant to its economy as wheat is to Saskatchewan, Ottawa would represent it more aggressively abroad.

Saskatchewan is more interested than Manitoba in national safety net provisions — and for a particular sector rather than for the economy as a whole. Saskatchewan is too small to be able to support its huge cereals farming sector single-handedly during bad or prolonged droughts. This is a direct consequence of both its concentration in wheat and its lack of international clout to protect that sector in world markets. It needs Canada because it cannot efficiently self-insure its provincial economy against outside risks.

Both Manitoba and Saskatchewan are below the national average income level, so both qualify for equalization payments to help maintain public services to national standards. For both, these payments represent an important part of provincial government revenue and an important commitment by Central Canada to justify some of the other federal policies (such as the National Policy) that have benefited Central Canada at the expense of the West.

Observed behavior suggests that both provinces are more concerned about equity than is the rest of Canada. This difference is revealed in several initiatives. Saskatchewan pioneered universal medical insurance. Manitoba was the first province to fold health insurance premiums into the income tax, making them at least as progressive as the income tax then was. More recently, Manitoba has broken out of the mold of the federal income tax to levy taxes on net income; even Conservative governments added several redistributive tax credits.

Efficiency

Like the two provinces further west, both Manitoba and Saskatchewan feel that efficiency in the delivery of public services is best achieved by sensitivity to local needs and circumstances — by leaving the matter to provincial or even municipal governments. Ottawa is simply too far away to understand properly the wishes of the recipients, the priorities of local jurisdictions, and the fiscal resources of provinces. In that sense, residents would prefer decentralized government. There are some spillovers from Manitoba and Saskatchewan to neighboring jurisdictions, but there are not many; the two provinces are too isolated for such externalities to be a big problem.

In the past, both provinces have seen the internal common market as a mixed blessing. Under the National Policy of the late 19th century, the West was intended as the sheltered market for Eastern Canadian production. Western response to this deal is revealed in its long-standing antipathy to the Canadian Pacific, the connecting link that made the National Policy work. When it comes to their own production and consumption, Western producers and consumers have long thought that north-south linkages make more sense than the trek across the Canadian Shield to southern Ontario. Primary producers of cereal crops are, of course, selling into an international market; their only concern is fair treaties to govern such trade and to keep the international playing field more or less level. Having a federal government unable or unwilling to accomplish and defend such a policy calls into serious question the gains from Confederation.

Meanwhile, Manitoba and Saskatchewan see the common market for capital leading to centralization of finance in Toronto (or

Vancouver in the future), with a consequent loss of control for themselves. Perhaps this centralization is inevitable, but the cooperative tradition of Saskatchewan coupled with Quebec's experience with the Caisses populaires Desjardins and the Caisse de dépôt et placement suggests that local financial control does make a difference. As for the common market for labor, there are already substantial barriers for professionals and skilled tradespeople. When one adds that other markets are distant and relocation costs are high, the promise of the common labor market makes less difference than one might expect from Toronto. Its major benefit is for the most mobile group — young people just starting out after completing their training, who can be absorbed by other provinces instead of being added to the local unemployment line if local demand is weak.

Thus, both Manitoba and Saskatchewan are ambivalent about entrenching economic union provisions in the Constitution. Although nobody is officially in favor of protectionism, many professional and business groups have a vested interest in provincial barriers to inflows of competitors. Despite the West's insistence that it must compete in global markets, for instance, its governments have been content to do most if not all of their tendering within the province. In too many other instances, the producers benefiting from the open markets of the economic union have been down East. Meanwhile, the union's benefit to consumers is neither compelling nor obvious, especially since highly visible crossborder prices are so much lower for most consumer durables.

In thinking about limitations on the role of government, citizens of Manitoba and Saskatchewan are likely to be less bothered than Easterners about big government. The rural sector's extensive cooperative experience in wheat pools, co-op stores, and credit unions has given them a long and satisfactory experience with collective action. And they have long relied on Crown corporations for essential utility services such as telephone and power. Although there is pressure to put some guarantee of private, capitalist property rights into the Constitution, Manitoba and Saskatchewan would undoubtedly reserve the right of government to intervene in a variety of ways. For instance, the farm sectors of both provinces are concerned that some level of government retain authority to prevent dock-workers in Thunder Bay and Prince Rupert from blocking the export of Prairie grain to world markets.

Conclusion

On the main issue of sovereignty versus renewed federalism, the less-affluent West has so little contact with Quebec that the majority support for keeping that province in Confederation must be based more on emotional desire to preserve the nation as symbol than on economic calculations of direct costs and benefits. The absence of obvious direct costs from Quebec's achieving sovereignty also accounts for some of the harder-line attitudes found in the West; like outputs, attitudes flourish where they are cheaper.

On issues of constitutional renewal, the less-affluent West has some interests in common with other provinces and some that differ. Political marginalization fuels demand for a form of regional representation better than first ministers' meetings. The Triple-E Senate proposal seems to have attracted the bulk of that demand.

Economic equity probably counts for more in a poorer, politically marginalized region than elsewhere; at least, economic inequity rankles longer. True economic equity would require much more than equalization payments. It would mean vigorous national lobbying in international grain-marketing councils (the equivalent of sending gunboats out to protect Maritime fishery resources). Closer to home, it would mean the federal government's cleaning up its patronage act in the regional allocation of its most important contracts.

Economic efficiency for the less-affluent West would mean less federal delivery of services but not necessarily less government in total. Residents have had by and large positive experiences with collective action in the past, and they support local and provincial governments. Although a strong central government may be *sine qua non* for preserving a Canadian common market for goods, labor, and capital, residents of Manitoba and Saskatchewan are ambivalent about many aspects of the concept as it has worked out in Canada. The result is lack of general support for strong central government control over the economy but no lack of specific support for a strong central government role in redistribution.

In closing, the picture that emerges is of a region with less at stake than the rest of the country in the two main items at risk: keeping Quebec in Canada and preserving a strong central government. Since residents have less at stake, they can be expected to tire of the discussion — especially the acrimonious parts — sooner than residents of Quebec and Ontario. Many are already at that point, with a year of discussion still to go.

It follows that Manitoba and Saskatchewan could follow one of two routes. Starkly stated, the first is to be satisfied under renewed federalism with the minimum recognition of distinct society status necessary to satisfy Quebec, coupled with Senate reform and minor changes in the economic union. The second is to respond emotionally to a long, confusing, and often acrimonious debate with the equivalent of shooting the messenger: digging in their heels to refuse any accommodation of Quebec and driving it out in order to end the discussion and get on with life in the less-affluent West.

Regional Perspectives:
Summary and Synthesis

John McCallum

The federal government redistributes large amounts of money from the richer provinces to the poorer provinces. Although the constitutional perspectives of Canada's regions differ for many reasons, there can be no doubt that differences relating to the redistributive role of the federal government are of central importance. Before summarizing the three studies that make up this volume, it may be useful to provide an overview of this redistributive effort by the federal government.

An Overview of Federal Government Fiscal Transfers

Some important features of the system are illustrated in Figures 1 and 2. Figure 1 plots each province's average relative income position over the 1980s against average per capita federal balances. Figure 2 shows trends since 1961 in relative income and federal balances for each of the four major regions.

Federal balances, taken from Statistics Canada's *Provincial Economic Accounts* (PEA), are defined as federal revenues raised in a province minus current federal expenditures in that province. Adjusted federal balances are equal to the actual balances plus an adjustment that serves to eliminate the effect of the federal deficit: the sum of adjusted federal balances for all provinces is equal to zero by definition.[1] A positive balance implies that the federal govern-

---

1 More precisely, the adjusted federal balance for, say, Manitoba is defined as federal revenues derived from Manitoba, minus current federal expenditures in...

Figure 1: **Adjusted Federal Balances and Per Capita Income, 1980–88**

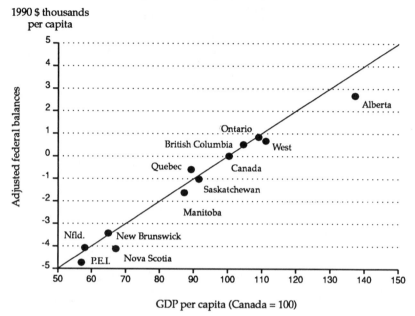

1990 $ thousands
per capita

GDP per capita (Canada = 100)

ment takes more money out of the province in revenues than it spends there — and conversely for a negative balance. Although several important caveats apply to the use of the PEA in this way, the large differences shown in Figures 1 and 2 do suggest a substantial amount of redistribution through the federal system. Moreover, a similar picture emerges if one replaces the federal balances with a measure of federal transfers to the provinces.[2] The main results can be summarized in the following points:

First, by almost any standard, the amount of redistribution is very large. Over the 1980–88 period, adjusted federal balances were

---

Note 1 - cont'd.

...Manitoba, minus Manitoba's share of the federal deficit. Here, the federal deficit is defined as the sum of federal balances in all provinces, and a province's share of the federal deficit is defined by its share in Canada's gross domestic product (GDP).

2 Transfers to a province are defined as total federal transfers to the relevant provincial government plus net receipts from unemployment insurance.

about –$4,000 per person per year (at 1990 prices) in the Atlantic region, compared with +$800 per person per year in both Ontario and Western Canada as a whole. The corresponding figure for Alberta was +$2,700. For the principal recipient region, Atlantic Canada, the adjusted balances amounted on average to some 28 percent of Atlantic Canada's GDP — and more than 30 percent of the GDP of Newfoundland and Prince Edward Island. For the donor regions, the net transfer amounted to around 3 percent of the GDP of Ontario and Western Canada and 8.6 percent of Alberta's. If one considers that industrialized countries have failed consistently to achieve their target of 1 percent of GDP in aid to the Third World, numbers of this magnitude clearly should be regarded as substantial.

Another way of looking at the situation reinforces this view. The large fiscal transfers to Atlantic Canada allow that region to import substantially more goods and services than it exports — and the converse is true for the donor provinces. This point is confirmed by the statistics from the PEA on net exports of goods and services over the 1980s: an average of –34 percent of Atlantic Canada's GDP, compared with +7.4 percent of Ontario's GDP and +12.4 percent of Alberta's. Again, these numbers are larger by an order of magnitude than the corresponding figures that one observes for sovereign nations. Thus — and notwithstanding statistical problems associated with the net export figures — one concludes that *the amount of redistribution through the federal system is very large.*

Second, the amount of the federal balance for a province is well explained by that province's relative income level (see Figure 1). By and large, then, the system has been doing what it is supposed to do in terms of direction: *the federal government has been redistributing from the rich provinces to the poor provinces.*

Third — and this is another point in favor of the federal effort — the system has also worked in the right direction over time. That is to say, *the amount of support from Ottawa has generally gone up during bad times and gone down during good times,* especially for the West. Western Canada was a significant net recipient of federal transfers until 1972 and a very substantial net payer during the 1973–85

Figure 2:   *Per Capita GDP and Net Federal*
                Transfers by Region, 1961–88

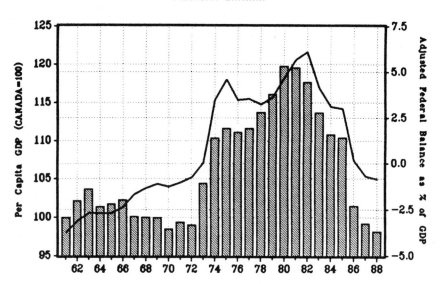

Western Canada

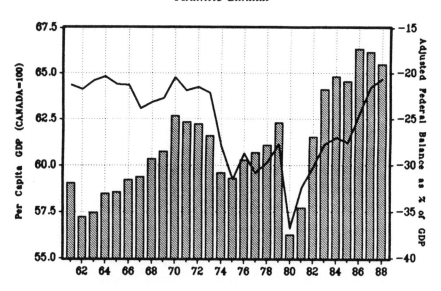

Atlantic Canada

Figure 2: *Per Capita GDP and Net Federal Transfers by Region, 1961–88 - continued*

Ontario

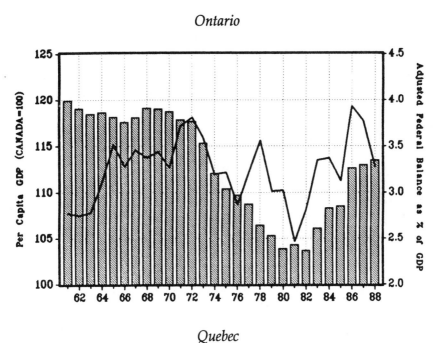

Quebec

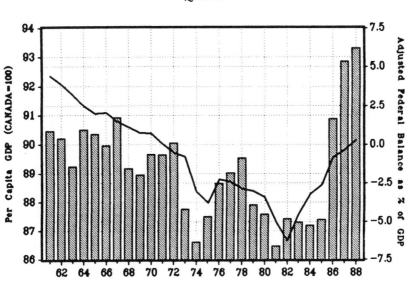

period, while net transfers to the region have been approximately zero since 1986 (see Figure 2). This pattern closely mirrors the sharp rise and subsequent decline in relative GDP in Western Canada. The figure also indicates that, over the past decade, there has been some catchup in relative income levels in Atlantic Canada, as well as some reduction in that region's dependence on federal transfers.

Finally, for the 1980–88 period, the redistributive pattern is particularly simple and may be expressed as follows. The system is approximately neutral *vis-à-vis* both Western Canada and Quebec, with the result that redistribution essentially takes two forms: from Ontario to Atlantic Canada; and from the "affluent" West (Alberta and British Columbia) to the "less-affluent" West (Saskatchewan and Manitoba).

This way of looking at the problem raises at least two questions that are addressed in this volume. First, it is not clear that Ontario will be able and/or willing to continue financing transfers to Atlantic Canada on the scale of recent years. As shown in Figure 2, while Ontario's lead over the rest of Canada in terms of per capita GDP has been declining over the past three decades, the share of Ontario's GDP devoted to subsidizing Atlantic Canada has, if anything, been rising. Moreover, while the data end in 1988, we know that Ontario has been especially hard hit by the 1990–91 recession and that the Ontario government's $10 billion deficit is about the same amount as the province's contribution to Atlantic Canada. The second issue concerns Western Canada: the large amounts of redistribution that occur within that region and the role of the federal system in helping to stabilize the large output fluctuations that are a characteristic of the region.

Atlantic Canada

As much as we may be willing to shake it cordially, we still fear the slap of Adam Smith's invisible hand.

– Doug May and Dane Rowlands

In their essay from the perspective of Atlantic Canada, Doug May and Dane Rowlands begin with the proposition that a "social" contract exists between the Atlantic provinces and the rest of the country. In that original contract, the provinces entered into an economic union (Section 121 of the *British North America Act*). The Maritime provinces, by entering the economic union, gave up their right to impose restrictions on the mobility of goods, labor, and capital. In return, they received guarantees from the federal government that economic development would be fostered in the region and that special fiscal transfers[3] would be made to their provincial governments to enable them to provide public services at levels closer to those of the richer provinces.

Over time, this economic union has been weakened by the imposition of trade barriers and policies to discourage migration. The hope that regional economic disparities would be overcome has not occurred. Instead, massive federal transfers to the region have created a dependency that all the Atlantic provinces would view as undesirable. May and Rowlands point out that any reduction in these transfers now could cause short-run pain and require substantial adjustment. To drive their point home, they analyze the implications of a reduction in federal transfer payments to the region, considering several adjustment mechanisms: lower wages, higher productivity, greater capital inflows to substitute for the reduction in federal transfers, and out-migration.

While acknowledging the likelihood of changes in the current system of transfers, May and Rowlands point out the potential difficulties of adjustment through any of the traditional market mechanisms. Partly because of the operation of a national labor market, it is difficult to reduce wages. Moreover, they argue, in a resource-based economy such as Atlantic Canada's, the major effect of productivity gains is to reduce jobs rather than to increase production. Traditional solutions, therefore, create the unwanted side effect of fewer jobs. In addition, it is most unlikely that higher private capital inflows would substitute for lower federal transfer payments,

3 New Brunswick entered with this understanding in 1867, while Nova Scotia received similar treatment in 1869. Term 29 of Newfoundland's Terms of Union with Canada explicitly contains such a provision.

and, since the Atlantic provinces are already at or near their credit limits, it is even less likely that increased borrowing by provincial governments could substitute for these transfers.

Finally, May and Rowlands argue that a substantial increase in out-migration, which has been occurring at levels similar to those in Western Canada in recent years, creates fears that the region will become a marginalized hinterland in which the loss of skilled labor reduces further the dream of self-reliance. Accompanying this process is the loss of culture and community identity along with political voice.

Having outlined Atlantic Canada's dependency on transfers from Ottawa, as well as the connection between large transfers and the maintenance of population, May and Rowlands go on to report the results of simulations that tend to support their argument. For example, if Canada were to break up and each province were to go its own way, then federal saving in Newfoundland would shift from current levels to zero. The May/Rowlands simulations indicate that, in this case, Newfoundland's population might drop by about 50 percent. In their "doomsday" scenario, which involves a breakup of Canada in combination with immigration restrictions imposed by the other provinces, population would not change much, but per capita income would drop by some 40 percent and the unemployment rate would go through the stratosphere to around 50 percent by 2000. May and Rowlands suggest that these numbers are likely to be "at least 30 percent higher" for Newfoundland than for Atlantic Canada as a whole.

The overall conclusion must be that any movement toward a more efficient economic union and a reduction in transfers will involve a period of difficult adjustment. All levels of government must cooperate to design policies to ease the process for those people who would be most affected. At the same time, while all parties recognize that the social contract that existed at the time of Confederation has since evolved, they must be clear about the manner in which constitutional reform rewrites this social contract. While many will see the social contract as part of wider regional issues with political overtones and tensions, May and Rowlands argue that: "The way Canada accommodates the aspirations of the Atlantic provinces will largely define how Canadians write the social contract among income classes as well."

Western Canada

In their contribution from the perspective of Western Canada, Edward Chambers and Michael Percy begin with a richly empirical analysis of the structure of the economy of that region. They focus on three of its major features:

*   *Its extreme dependence on a small number of exported commodities.* For three of the four Western provinces, two or three commodities account for more than one-half of total exports: lumber, wood pulp, and coal for British Columbia; petroleum and natural gas for Alberta; and wheat, petroleum, and potash for Saskatchewan. Manitoba has a much more diversified economy.
*   *Its extreme susceptibility to harassment by U.S. protectionism.* This is the result of the specialization and geographic concentration of Western Canada's exports.
*   *Its extreme volatility.* This "boom-or-bust" characteristic is also a result of the region's dependence on a small number of resource-based exports. Chambers and Percy document this volatility in a number of areas, including export prices, housing prices, population, gross domestic product, investment, and personal income. Generally speaking, Alberta's economy is the most volatile, followed by British Columbia's and Saskatchewan's. Manitoba's economy, being much more diversified, is much more stable.[4]

Because of this economic structure, Chambers and Percy argue, Western Canada benefits from membership in the Canadian economic union in two important ways. First, Canada has more market

---

4 As Norman Cameron, Derek Hum, and Wayne Simpson note in their contribution to this volume, Manitoba's growth is "slow but steady" in bad times, and "steady but slow" in good times.

power in international trade than would an independent Western Canada. As an example, Chambers and Percy suggest that if the West had been an independent entity, the softwood lumber dispute of 1986 probably would have ended with a U.S. countervail duty, rather than the temporary export tax levied by the federal government.

The West's second major economic benefit from Confederation lies in the potential for pooling risks across a country of 26 million people. The economic stabilization and insurance aspects of an economic union are crucial for a region with a highly volatile economy. Labor mobility has become an important adjustment mechanism and, as Chambers and Percy point out, the alternative to interregional migration is greater variability in either income or unemployment. Moreover, an independent West would be less able to provide economic stabilization because it would not have the diversified tax base on which the federal government can draw today.

This is not to deny that politicians in an independent West would *try* to diversify their economy; indeed, Chambers and Percy present strong evidence that they would face intense pressures to reduce volatility by engaging in provincial diversification policies. Such policies, however, would be undesirable from an economic standpoint, since they would reduce incomes and economic efficiency.

It is important to note the difference between the *potential* for stabilization and *actual* stabilization as carried out by the federal government in recent decades. Chambers and Percy suggest that exchange-rate movements in recent years have often amplified Western booms and exacerbated contractions, and that federal transfer programs should be more responsive to the Western commodity cycle and less directed toward maintaining the current distribution of Canada's population. Similarly, they argue, federal policies should promote labor mobility and market-based mechanisms of regional adjustment. In short:

> Shifting the focus of the institutions of Confederation from maintaining the status quo in the spatial distribution of economic activity and population in Canada to dealing with the consequences of economic volatility would improve the well-

being of all residents of Canada, not just those in Western Canada, and would contribute to increasing the surplus of the economic union.

This market-based view is not only diametrically opposed to the vision from Atlantic Canada as exemplified by May and Rowlands; it also may encounter some resistance in the less-affluent West of Manitoba and Saskatchewan.

The "Affluent" and "Less-Affluent" West

Norman Cameron, Derek Hum, and Wayne Simpson provide a thoughtful description of the constitutional perspectives of the less-affluent West. They emphasize strong attachments to *political equality* — hence their preference for a Triple-E Senate; *economic equity* — hence the importance they attach to equalization payments and farm assistance to Saskatchewan, and their opposition to regional "patronage", as illustrated by the CF-18 episode; and *economic efficiency*. On this last point, Cameron, Hum, and Simpson favor decentralization to provincial governments and, while acknowledging the importance of unimpeded labor mobility, they express a certain nervousness about the centralization of finance in Toronto that results from a common market for capital.

The less-affluent West apparently is less bothered about "big government" than is the East — although it would like to see fewer *federal* services being delivered. The unabashedly promarket stance of Chambers and Percy — particularly their opposition to policies designed to maintain the status quo in terms of the spatial distribution of Canada's population and economic activity — likely would induce nervousness in the less-affluent West.

Conflicting Visions of Canada

In addition to the three studies just described, this volume contains comments by the West on the East (Chambers and Percy on May and

Rowlands) and by the East on the West (Rowlands on Chambers and Percy). The reader can scarcely avoid being struck by the sharp differences in regional perspectives and by the difficulties the federal government is likely to face in trying to reconcile these differences.

On the one hand, according to the Atlantic vision described by May and Rowlands, large federal transfers to the region are seen as one side of an unalterable social contract. Or, in the words of Chambers and Percy: "In this Atlantic view, the rest of Canada is nothing more than a foreign-aid donor without the right to seek structural adjustments by the recipient."

May and Rowlands do suggest that young Newfoundlanders do not welcome this dependency. They also point to the entrepreneurial talents of Atlantic Canadians — but only in terms of their adroit response to the opportunities arising from the unemployment insurance program. As Chambers and Percy suggest, the paper by May and Rowlands makes depressing reading because they offer little hope that Atlantic Canada will ever escape from its current state of dependency. To a lesser degree, Cameron, Hum, and Simpson, writing from the less-affluent West, also see federal assistance as part of a "social contract" or *quid pro quo* — in this case justified by "some of the other federal policies (such as the National Policy) that have benefited Central Canada at the expense of the West."

Against this "social contract" or "entitlement" view of Canada, Chambers and Percy favor a market system based primarily on insurance and stabilization rather than preserving the present distribution of Canada's population. This difference, as Rowlands emphasizes in his comment, "may well be the fundamental conflict between Atlantic Canadians and Western Canadians with respect to the Constitution." He could have added that the less-affluent West might side with Atlantic Canada on this issue, while Quebec, despite its have-not status, appears closer to the market-oriented view of Alberta. This leaves Ontario, whose economic interest clearly lies in the direction of Atlantic Canada's reduced dependency, but whose government may have a strong philosophical commitment to regional equalization.

Another striking contrast is between the large amounts of federal redistribution to the poorer regions — as described above and shown in Figure 1 — and the perceptions of our writers from the recipient regions. For example, Cameron, Hum, and Simpson describe Manitoba and Saskatchewan as politically powerless, and they speak of the resentment felt toward special economic advantages received by Quebec — of which the CF-18 contract is a notable case. Yet, in recent years those two provinces have received net benefits approaching 10 percent of their respective GDPs, compared with less than 1 percent for Quebec — at least, as measured by the adjusted federal balances presented here. Rowlands, on the other hand, notes that Atlantic Canadians view extensive out-migration as a "social scourge that is, in some sense, unique to the region." It is a fact, however, that over the past three decades the population of Atlantic Canada has increased by more than the population of either Manitoba or Saskatchewan.

In conclusion, while the studies offer interesting insights and perspectives, they also indicate that much work remains to be done. For Atlantic Canada, is mass out-migration really the only possible response to reduced federal financing? Are there not concrete actions or policies that could be adopted to reduce dependency and foster autonomous regional development?[5] For Western Canada, while a federalist argument coming out of the (affluent) West is certainly welcome, it is also true, as Rowlands points out, that "the strength of [Chambers' and Percy's]...argument lies in the potential for gains in the future, rather than on any gains that we have demonstrated an ability to exploit in the past." How will renewed federalism increase our ability to exploit these gains? Such basic questions remain unanswered.

---

5 For a paper that begins to address some of these issues, see Atlantic Provinces Economic Council, "Atlantic Economic Cooperation: An Exploration of the Concept, Its Benefits, and Costs" (Background paper prepared for the 1991 Annual Conference of the Atlantic Provinces Economic Council, Dartmouth, Nova Scotia, June 11, 1991, Mimeographed).

The Contributors

Norman Cameron is Professor of Economics in the Faculty of Arts, Adjunct Professor in the Faculty of Management, and Fellow of St. John's College, all at the University of Manitoba. His research interests were originally in the Soviet economy, but they have since shifted to matters macroeconomic, financial, and Canadian. His most recent work is on the Canadian financial system and monetary policy.

E.J. Chambers is Professor of Marketing and Economic Analysis at the University of Alberta, and Director of the Western Centre for Economic Research, which is co-sponsored by the University of Alberta and the C.D. Howe Institute. Dr. Chambers has published in the areas of economic and business development, macroeconomics, and regional problems.

Derek Hum is currently Professor of Economics at the University of Manitoba. He was formerly research director of Mincome, an experimental test of negative taxation sponsored by the governments of Canada and Manitoba. He specializes in social policy, labor, and intergovernmental relations.

John McCallum is Chair and Professor of Economics at McGill University, Montreal, and, effective June 1992, Dean of the Faculty of Arts. His research interests have focused on applied macroeconomics, cross-country comparisons, and Canadian economic policy and history. He is currently editing the C.D. Howe Institute's *The Canada Round*, a series of studies on the economics of Canada's constitutional crisis.

Doug May is Professor of Economics at Memorial University of Newfoundland, St. John's. He is currently President of the Atlantic Canada

Economics Association and a Director of the John Deutsch Institute for the Study of Economic Policy at Queen's University, Kingston. Dr. May was recently appointed to Newfoundland's Constitutional Committee by Premier Clyde Wells. His current research interests involve international competitiveness and regional development.

M.B. Percy is Professor of Economics and Associate Dean of Arts (Planning) at the University of Alberta. He has published extensively in the areas of Canadian economic development, resource management, and regional economic policy. Dr. Percy is currently involved in a major project assessing the economic implications for Alberta of alternate constitutional scenarios.

Dane Rowlands is a graduate student in the Department of Economics at the University of Toronto, and is currently on a leave of absence from Memorial University of Newfoundland.

Wayne Simpson is Professor of Economics at the University of Manitoba. He has worked for the federal government and the Economic Council of Canada, and his research interests include labor economics, applied econometrics, and urban economics.

Members of the
C.D. Howe Institute[*]

[*] The views expressed in this publication are those of the authors, and do not necessarily reflect the opinions of the Institute's members.

E. Kendall Cork
Corporation du Groupe La Laurentienne
Coscan Development Corporation
William J. Cosgrove
Co-Steel Inc.
Pierre Côté
The Counsel Corporation
J.G. Crean
Crédit Lyonnais Canada
Crestbrook Forest Industries Ltd.
John Crispo
Crown Life Insurance Company Limited
Hugh A. Curtis
Cyanamid Canada Inc.
Deloitte & Touche
Desjardins, Ducharme
Desmarais Family Foundation
Robert Després
John H. Dickey
William A. Dimma
Iain St. C. Dobson
Dofasco Inc.
The Dominion of Canada General
    Insurance Company
Domtar Inc.
Donohue Inc.
Dow Chemical Canada Inc.
Du Pont Canada Inc.
Edper Investments Ltd.
The Empire Life Insurance Company
Encor Inc.
Energy & Chemical Workers Union
H.E. English
Ernst & Young
Falconbridge Limited
Ronald J. Farano, Q.C.
Federal Industries Ltd.
Field & Field Perraton Masuch
First Boston Canada
First Marathon Securities Limited
Fishery Products International Limited
Ford Motor Company of Canada, Limited
Formula Growth Limited
Four Seasons Hotels Limited
GSW Inc.
Gaz Métropolitain, Inc.
General Electric Canada Inc.

General Motors of Canada Limited
Gluskin Sheff + Associates Inc.
The Great-West Life Assurance Company
Morton Gross
Le Groupe Commerce, compagnie
    d'assurances
Le Groupe Secor Inc.
Groupe Sobeco Inc.
Gulf Canada Resources Limited
H. Anthony Hampson
C. Malim Harding Foundation
Hawker Siddeley Canada Inc.
Hewlett-Packard (Canada) Ltd.
Home Oil Company Limited
Gordon Homer
Honeywell Limited
Hongkong Bank of Canada
Hydro-Québec
IBM Canada Ltd.
Imasco Limited
Imperial Oil Limited
Inco Limited
The Independent Petroleum Association
    of Canada
Inland Cement Limited
The Insurance Bureau of Canada
Interprovincial Pipe Line Company
The Investors Group
IPSCO Incorporated
Tsutomu Iwasaki
John A. Jacobson
Jarislowsky, Fraser & Company
Robert Johnstone
John Labatt Limited
LAC Minerals Ltd.
R.William Lawson
Jacques Lefebvre
David Lewis
Gérard Limoges
Daniel Lobb
London Life Insurance Company
Pierre Lortie
J.W. (Wes) MacAleer
McCallum Hill Companies
MacDonald, Dettwiler & Associates Ltd.
Robert M. MacIntosh
McKinsey & Company

Maclab Enterprises
James Maclaren Industries Inc.
Maclean-Hunter Limited
Charles McMillan
McMillan, Binch
MacMillan Bloedel Limited
William Mackness
Manufacturers Hanover Bank of Canada
The Manufacturers Life Insurance
Company
Maple Leaf Foods Inc.
Georg Marais
Maritime Telegraph & Telephone
Company, Limited
Marsh & McLennan Limited
The Mercantile and General Reinsurance
Company of Canada
William M. Mercer Limited
Merck Frosst Canada Inc.
Ronald H. Meredith-Jones
Miles Canada Inc.
Les Minoteries Ogilvie Ltée.
Robert Mitchell Inc.
Mitsui & Co. (Canada) Ltd.
The Molson Companies Limited
Monsanto Canada Inc.
Montréal Trust Company of Canada
Moore Corporation Limited
The Mutual Life Assurance Company of
Canada
NCR Canada Ltd.
National Westminster Bank of Canada
Nesbitt Thomson Deacon
Noranda Forest Inc.
Noranda Inc.
North American Life Assurance Company
North Canadian Oils Limited
Northern Telecom Limited
Northwood Pulp and Timber Limited
NOVA Corporation of Alberta
Ontario Hydro
The Oshawa Group Limited
PanCanadian Petroleum Limited
Peat Marwick Thorne
Lucie Pépin
Petro-Canada Inc.
Les Placements T.A.L. Ltée.
Placer Dome Inc.

David A. Potts
Power Corporation of Canada
Pratt & Whitney Canada Inc.
Price Waterhouse & Co.
J. Robert S. Prichard
Procor Limited
ProGas Limited
Provigo Inc.
Quebec and Ontario Paper Company
Limited
RBC Dominion Securities Inc.
Redpath Industries Limited
Simon S. Reisman
Henri Remmer
Retail Council of Canada
Grant L. Reuber
R.T. Riley
Robin Hood Multifoods Inc.
Rogers Communications Inc.
Rothschild Canada Inc.
The Royal Bank of Canada
Royal Insurance Company of Canada
Royal Trust
St. Lawrence Cement Inc.
Sandwell Inc.
Saskoil
Guylaine Saucier
André Saumier
The Hon. Maurice Sauvé
Sceptre Investment Counsel
Sceptre Resources Limited
Dick Schmeelk
ScotiaMcLeod Inc.
Sears Canada Inc.
Hugh D. Segal
Sharwood and Company
Shell Canada Limited
Sherritt Gordon Limited
Sidbec-Dosco Inc.
Smith, Lyons, Torrance, Stevenson &
Mayer
Le Soleil
Southam Inc.
Derek J. Speirs
Philip Spencer, Q.C.
Standard Life Assurance Company
Stikeman, Elliott, Advocates

Strategico Inc.
Sun Life Assurance Company of Canada
Suncor Inc.
Swiss Bank Corporation (Canada)
Teck Corporation
Laurent Thibault
Thomson Newspapers Limited
3M Canada Inc.
The Toronto Dominion Bank
Toronto Star Newspaper Limited
The Toronto Stock Exchange
TransAlta Utilities Corporation
TransCanada PipeLines Limited
Trimac
Trizec Corporation Ltd.

Robert J. Turner
Unilever Canada Inc.
Urgel Bourgie Limitée
Manon Vennat
VIA Rail Canada Inc.
J.H. Warren
West Fraser Timber Co. Ltd.
Westcoast Energy Inc.
George Weston Limited
Alfred G. Wirth
M.K. Wong & Associates Ltd.
Wood Gundy Limited
Xerox Canada Inc.
Zurich Life Insurance of Canada

Honorary Members

G. Arnold Hart
David Kirk
Paul H. Leman

A.M. Runciman
J. Ross Tolmie, Q.C.

Publications in "The Canada Round"

The Economics of Constitutional Renewal

How Shall We Govern the Governor? A Critique of the Governance of the Bank of Canada, The Canada Round 1, by David E.W. Laidler (38 pp.; May 1991).

In Praise of Renewed Federalism, The Canada Round 2, by Thomas J. Courchene (102 pp.; July 1991). This publication is also available in French.

From East and West : Regional Views on Reconfederation, The Canada Round 6, by Norman Cameron, E.J. Chambers, Derek Hum, John McCallum, Doug May, M.B. Percy, Dane Rowlands, and Wayne Simpson (122 pp.; December 1991).

(Forthcoming)

The Division of Spending and Taxing Powers, by Irene Ip and Jack Mintz, with John Richards, Jean-Michel Cousineau, Robin Boadway, André Raynauld, and Claude Forget.

The Social Charter, by Lars Osberg, Shelly Phipps, Havi Echenberg, Arthur Milner, John Myles, John Richards, and William B.P. Robson.

Fiscal Policy: Deficits and Regional Coordination, by Herbert Grubel, with William Scarth, Douglas Purvis, and Jan Winter.

Resource Mobility and the Economic Union, by Fred Lazar, David Brown, and Daniel Schwanen.

The European Community Model and the Canadian Constitutional Debate, by G. Bruce Doern.

Summary and Synthesis, by Richard Lipsey and John McCallum